W9-DBI-371

LADIES
OR
GENTLEMEN?

THE MAN-WOMAN

From a print of the XVIIIth century suggested by the career of the
Chevalier D'Eon

LADIES
OR
GENTLEMEN?

Women Who Posed as Men and
Men Who Impersonated Women

C.J.S. THOMPSON

Dorset Press
New York

Originally published as *The Mysteries of Sex*

This edition published by Dorset Press,
a division of Barnes & Noble, Inc.

1993 Dorset Press

ISBN 1-56619-199-8

Printed and bound in the United States of America

M 9 8 7 6 5 4 3 2 1

CONTENTS

PART ONE

WOMEN WHO POSED AS MEN

CONTENTS

PART TWO

MEN WHO IMPERSONATED WOMEN

PART THREE

CLAIMANTS TO ROYAL AND OTHER TITLES

LIST OF ILLUSTRATIONS

Women who Posed as Men

SOME may think that it is hardly correct to apply the word 'impersonator' to many of the strange characters described in the following pages.

According to the *New English Dictionary* an impersonator is 'one who plays a part,' and the act of impersonating is 'to represent in a bodily form or to invest with an actual personality.'

In cases of sex impersonation, however, it is necessary to give the word a wider interpretation, for it will be seen that the impersonators rarely 'represent in a bodily form,' and usually had some specific reason for masquerading as individuals of the opposite sex.

It is in this wider sense that the word is used here : it will be apparent that a woman may dress, act, and live the life of a man, and that a man may adopt the manner and appearance of a woman, without playing the part of a particular person.

In some of the earlier stories recounted, I have endeavoured to retain the quaint and stilted phraseology of the periods in which the individuals lived.

I wish to acknowledge my indebtedness to the works of O. P. Gilbert and M. M. Dowie in connexion with some of the biographies.

IMPERSONATION may be said to spring from that inherent urge for imitation in the human race evident from very early times, which led men to assume the garments used by women and women to masquerade in men's apparel. The article in ancient Hebrew law that ' the woman shall not wear that which pertaineth unto a man, neither shall a man put on a woman's garment, for all that do so are an abomination to the Lord God,' shows that such practices were known at least four thousand years before the Christian era.

The Old Testament story tells us how Jacob attempted to deceive his blind father by impersonating his brother Esau, and describes later how Saul disguised himself and put on ' other raiment ' to deceive the witch of Endor.

From the early Assyrian cuneiform tablets it is evident that some of their kings affected feminine arts, and it is recorded that Assurbanipal (668–626 B.C.) not only painted his face with vermilion and employed cosmetics lavishly, but even adopted women's attire.

Later on, in the time of the Roman Empire, we have evidence of the same effeminate spirit among the Cæsars, who are said to have been fond of arraying themselves in female robes, while some of the Emperors found delight in playing the woman.

In considering the subject it is first necessary to try to discover what motives gave rise to these sex vagaries, and in investigating this the pathological condition of the individual is also of some importance.

The predisposing cause and origin of the impulse is not easy to explain, for it is both pathological and psychological. Scientific investigators claim that sex penetrates the whole person and is normally determined before birth.

Probably every individual is made up of mixed masculine and feminine elements variously combined. It was thought at one time that a woman was a woman because of her physiological organization alone, but it has since been shown that this is not the case. Femininity itself is dependent on all the internal secretions.

The general tissues of the body possess the potency of developing the characters of either sex under the stimulus of the special complex of sex hormones which they receive. 'Thus,' says Havelock Ellis, 'when the male hormone appears later than usual, some form of inter-sexuality results and the later its appearance the more femaleness.'

Crew declares that the degree of abnormality will be determined by the time at which the male sex hormone becomes operative. This may help to explain why an individual who appears female in early life assumes male characteristics at sexual maturity.

Since every person contains the physical germs of the opposite sex, it is reasonable to suppose that he or she may also contain the psychic germs. It is said indeed that all animals also contain the elements of both sexes in some degree.

The term *Eonism* has been given to the condition of an individual who identifies himself or herself with the opposite sex, not merely in dress but in general tastes, in ways of acting, and in emotional disposition. Many instances of this condition will be found in the following pages, such as the cases of the Chevalier D'Eon and the Abbé de Choisy among men, and of Lady Hester Stanhope and others of the opposite sex.

In some cases the ordinary life of the individual may present no startling or unusual traits and may seem quite normally masculine. With men, they are often devoted to their wives, and their secret ideals are generally unsuspected.

It is not all who develop the desire to adopt the clothes of the opposite sex, but when they do they usually achieve complete success in assuming feminine or masculine tastes and ways.

It is well known that during the reproductive period remarkable changes in the sex-character of women may be brought about. In some cases the voice, previously high-pitched, may become harsher and deeper in tone, and the woman, formerly gentle and amiable, may become aggressive and rough.

Two American investigators recently endeavoured to devise a test of mental masculinity and femininity, which they based on actual differences between male and female groups ranging in age from early adolescence to old age. They observed that psychologists, psychiatrists, and sociologists are generally agreed that the effective life of a woman tends to differ in a number of ways from that of a man. Man is supposed to be more given to anger and a woman to the sympathetic emotions.

With regard to the impersonation of one sex by another, it was observed that too close attachment to the mother in early life was a factor in many cases and that some defection of the endocrine balance may account for this.

The most pronounced age of masculinity is youth, and men become more feminine with age. It is well known that the average normal boy makes every effort to prevent his behaviour and appearance from being effeminate, but the feminine personality of some men is apparent in their personal fastidiousness, attention to dress, preference for feminine occupations, and fondness of sentiment in plays, films, and literature. On the other hand, masculine women prefer male pursuits and like striding about in men's top-boots, breeches, and jackets ; they enjoy leadership, admire physical courage, and are interested in adventure, travel, hardships, and warfare.

We are told that youth is the period of enthusiastic energy, even of violence, and also that it is the age of criminality. On the other hand age and maturity develop femininity in tastes and general interests. As an instance, some elderly men have been known to delight in feminine surroundings, and one man of over seventy years old had his bedroom elaborately decorated in pink, white, and gold. Over his gilded bed golden cupids were suspended, and the canopy was hung with pink silk curtains, while bows of pink ribbon were tied on the lace-edged pillows. On the walls were hung pictures of beautiful women, and his dressing-table was furnished with an assortment of face-creams, cosmetics, and perfumes, which would have delighted the heart of a woman of fashion.

The homosexual not only accentuates any feminine qualities he may already possess, such as a high-pitched voice, but also attempts to imitate women in speech, walk, and mannerisms, and from early childhood is usually characterized by an inversion of interests, attitudes, and activities.

The practice of one sex assuming the costume of the other formed part of the old English custom of ' mumming,' at one time common at the Christmas season. The men dressed themselves in women's clothes and the women donned the men's, and thus arrayed, they went from ' one neighbour's house to another making merry in their disguises.' This ancient custom is believed to have originated in the festival days added to the early Saturnalia. It was condemned by the Synod of Trullus, who decreed that no man should go clothed in a woman's garment nor any woman in a man's. It was prohibited in the time of Henry VIII, and persons disguising themselves in such apparel were ordered to be arrested as vagabonds and committed to gaol for three months.

Impersonation was frequent on the stage from ancient times, and in the early seventeenth century it was common for young men to play the part of women—and they did it with great success. One of the stars of the time was Nathaniel Field, who performed in female parts at the Globe and Blackfriars' theatres and played opposite Burbage in some of Beaumont and Fletcher's dramas.

Field, at the age of twenty-three, is described as having a peculiarly smooth and feminine look and no whiskers. Another famous actor was Alexander Goffe, who played women's parts from the age of twelve and was known as the 'woman-actor of Blackfriars.' Kynaston and James Nokes were equally popular as female impersonators, and the last named is said never to have completely abandoned petticoats. Even to-day the impersonation of other artists by imitators is a popular 'turn' in the variety theatres.

Instances of metamorphosis are constantly occurring in both Europe and America. One case that came to light recently in the United States was that of a young man who dressed for three months as a woman. He had masqueraded first as a Russian princess, and later took a post as a waitress in a bar. Another case was that of a girl of twenty-three years of age who was arrested by the police wearing men's clothes. She declared she had always wanted to be a boy and from the time she was eight had always been dressed as a boy and called 'Harry.'

The most puzzling cases of impersonation are the physiological or hermaphrodite types, of which some extraordinary instances are on record. There is the one of Catherine or Charles Hoffman, who was born in 1824 and considered a female until she reached the age of forty. According to her own account, when she was fourteen she had all the instincts of a woman, which continued until she reached the age of forty-six, when they completely changed to those of a man. Another was that of Marie-Madeline Lefort, who was born in 1815. When she was sixteen she developed a moustache and whiskers, and decided to dress as a man. At nineteen, all the instincts of a woman returned and she then disappeared until 1864. One day a person with a long, grey beard whose sex to the eye was unmistakable, came as a patient to the Hôtel Dieu, in Paris, asking for treatment for pleurisy. He was admitted but died from the disease shortly afterwards. When the body was examined it was revealed that the supposed man had all the essential organs of a female.

Another baffling case was that of Marie-Dorothée ; although she was given a feminine name, her sex could not be defined. She dressed as a woman until she was twenty-three and was then examined by five experts, two of whom declared she was a girl, while three affirmed she was a boy. In 1803 she possessed certificates of birth of both sexes. She is described as being small in build and stature with an effeminate voice, but having no beard or hair on the face. Marc, a scientific investigator of the time, came to the conclusion that it was impossible for anyone to determine if she was of one sex or the other.

A more recent and remarkable case of double change of sex was reported from Athens towards the end of 1937. A thirteen-year-old girl named Georgette, who was at a boarding-school, developed masculine tendencies, and a medical man, after examining her, declared she was a boy. Her dress was changed accordingly and she was renamed

George. A few years later George fell in love with one of his former girl friends and they were contemplating marriage when a further change became noticeable in the proposed bridegroom. He was examined by a professor of gynæcology in the University of Athens, and, after an operation, he declared George was definitely a girl ; so once again the victim of these changes took the name of Georgette.

Another curious case is related by Lilian T. Mowrer, in her recent book, *Journalist's Wife*, concerning ' Hermann W——, a painter, and his wife G——, who designed covers for *La Vie Parisienne*,' whom she knew in Paris.

' Hermann,' she says, ' was a gentle creature whose artistic efforts were restricted to copying masterpieces in the Louvre. But his fate was strikingly original, for fifteen years later he turned into a woman and died of pneumonia just before giving birth to a child.'

In attempting to analyse the impulses or motives that have actuated both men and women in impersonating the opposite sex, it is evident that in some cases they were victims of circumstances. But the chief causes of their action among women, apart from the physiological, appear to have been a spirit of adventure, ambition, a psychological desire for domination and to play the man, or a criminal desire to obtain money or property. Among men, insensate vanity, egoism, homosexuality, and the acquisition of property appear to have been the chief impulses. In this country women who pose as men are usually of two types : viz. those who adopt the dress of men as a temporary disguise, perhaps for criminal purposes or in order to live as crooks, and those who not only assume male attire but live and act like men. As the law stands it is an offence for a man publicly to assume women's clothing, but it is not an offence for a woman to dress as a man so long as she does not contravene the law.

III

MARY FRITH,
OR 'MOLL CUTPURSE'

AMONG the strange and notorious characters known in London life in the mid-seventeenth century was Mary Frith, popularly called 'Moll Cutpurse' on account of her dexterity in picking pockets. During her varied career she became in turn a practitioner of astrology and fortune-telling, a thief, a pickpocket, and a 'fence,' or receiver of stolen goods.

She claimed to be half man and half woman, and there seems little doubt, if we can believe her own confession, that she was of the hermaphrodite type.

She was born in Barbican, at the upper end of Aldersgate Street, London, in 1584, her father being a shoemaker by trade and reputably an honest, hard-working man. Her mother treated her as a girl in infancy and was devoted to her. As she grew up she developed masculine instincts and became boisterous and rough : she would only take part in boys' games and pastimes and could not be persuaded to play or to associate with girls. Her chief delight was fighting with cudgels or the quarter-staff and cracking a head or two in a fight, while she could run, jump, or wrestle with the best of her boy playmates. On the death of her mother, there was no one who could control her unruly temper, consequently she ran wild and got her father into constant trouble. She is described at this time as 'a very towrig and rumpscuttle.'

Her uncle on her mother's side was a clergyman of whom she stood in some awe. He was a jolly and

19

easygoing parson and was known as one of the few who refused to take tithes from his parishioners. He did his best to restrain Mary's wild proclivities but finding his endeavours in that direction were of little avail, gave up trying to reform her.

She developed into a strong and sturdy young person who found a quarter-staff nearer to her hand than a distaff. Her greatest ambition was to be thought and treated as a man, and with this idea she abandoned girls' clothes for those of a youth. She had a great distaste for domestic duties and loathed looking after children ; consequently, no man liked or came near her. All her characteristics were masculine, for we are told that ' she never had green-sickness, that epidemical of maidens, never changed her complexion, and was never known to blush or go pale.'

Without restraint she made many doubtful acquaintances and among them some of the so-called astrologers and fortune-tellers who flourished in London at that time. These quack practitioners not only forecast the future and the fortunes of their customers but even prophesied the winner in a race, as instanced by W. Baynham, who was to be found at the ' Blew Ball in St. Andrew's Street, the corner house over against the upper end of St. Martin's-lane, next the Seven Dials, St. Giles,' who advertised he could tell ' Which shall win in Horse or Foot races.' Others claimed to be able to reveal where lost or stolen valuables were to be discovered and how they could be restored. Mary lost no time in acquiring the latter faculty, which she turned to account with considerable profit later on, as well as a general knowledge of the fortune-teller's art.

The story of her career is told in a quaint little book, purporting to be her ' diary ' and printed in 1662. She first tells us how on finding herself to be half woman and half man, she devised a dress that

CATALINA DE ERAUSO

(Engraved from her portrait by Pacheco, 1630.)

MARY FRITH, KNOWN AS 'MOLL CUTPURSE'

(From an eighteenth-century engraving.)

CHRISTIAN DAVIES, THE WOMAN DRAGOON
(From an eighteenth-century engraving.)

would be suitable for either sex. It consisted of a man's doublet, which she wore on the upper part of her body, and a woman's skirt to cover her legs. This she sometimes exchanged for breeches.

'I beheld myself,' she declares, 'more obnoxious to my fate and to have a greater quarrel with that than the world can have with me. The world consists of the cheats and the cheated.'

Mary resolved to be one of the former class, whereby she was likely to get hold of more money, and says : ' my devices were all my own spinning.' The following story illustrates her cunning and ingenuity. Being friendly with several expert thieves she formed a plan by means of which she could restore stolen property to their owners and, at the same time, fill her own pocket. She took a house two doors from the Globe Tavern in Fleet Street, near the Conduit, where she made it known she could be consulted as to the whereabouts of lost or stolen property. Acting as a ' fence ' or receiver of the valuables acquired by her thieving friends, she was thus able to inform any inquirers who came to consult her how their stolen property could be restored to them on receipt of a suitable reward, which was generally forthcoming. Thus in the upper rooms of her house she gathered a vast store of stolen property and jewellery of one kind or another.

To extend her activities she decided to join a band of what she calls ' land pyrates,' and resolved to learn their art thoroughly. Her training appears to have been carried out in quite a scientific manner. ' On my admission to their circle,' she says, ' I was examined as to my fitness and capacity for being a member. They viewed my hands to see if they were naturally fitted for the trade. I learnt that the best signs and marks of a happy and industrious hand is a long middle-finger, equally suited with what they call "the fool's or first finger." . . . Above all things they abhor a clumsy fat finger, as apt to slip the "coal," which they put for the money, and not carry it cleverly, and they hate a bungler as much as a dunce. They have several forms or sorts of pickpockets. They have one fellow always in company when they go about this employment whom they call a "bulk," who makes some quarrel in the street or obstructs a person while the "whipsters" do the feat.

'I had no great promising symptoms of a lucky mercurial in my fingers, for they had not been used to any slight or fine work, but I was judged by these "palmisters" to be very well qualified to be a receiver of their fortunate achievements.' Her instructors were evidently competent and experienced in the craft, for she remarks, 'no surgeon or doctor of physick could read a learned anatomy lecture of the nerves and arteries of the hand better than these cutting empiricks.

'Once established I had very good correspondence with those grandees of the function of thieving, the blades and bucks of the Highway, who having had from their inferior tribe repute of my equitable dealing . . . But,' she concludes, 'I never harboured a felon under my roof and by this means I kept myself free from all manner of inspection.'

But in spite of her love for fortune-telling, Mary expresses great contempt for the astrologers or 'figure-flingers,' as she calls them, and in this showed more sense than many people do to-day. 'It was not universally practised,' she says, 'since the ominous death of Dr. Lamb who was stoned by the apprentices in the street. People were not so fond of the stars and their cheaty secretaries as to consult them often. . . . Nothing but losses and the certainty of recovery of them engaged my office. Of the Jack Puddings of this reformation I never abhorred any more than Hugh Peters and William Lilly, the very disgrace of our art and profession, with their lying wonders and juggling deceits and impudent falsehoods.' She complains of the competition of foreigners who, she says, ' had all the trade, while the natives had nothing to do,' but in relieving pockets of purses Mary had no equal.

Her favourite fields of operation were Covent Garden and the neighbourhood of the theatres, where, through her successful depredations, she became known as ' Moll Cutpurse.'

Captain Hind and Richard Hannam, the notorious highwaymen, were among her friends, and it is said that she once robbed General Fairfax on Hounslow Heath, shot him in the arm, and killed two horses which his servants were riding. For this outrage she was sent to Newgate, but procured her release by paying the General two thousand pounds.

In her lively diary, which is written with a sense of humour, she describes an adventure when she was nearly abducted.

' I was hardly twenty, and was just beginning to view the manners and customs of the age, poor silly wench that I was. Under pretence of a Fair and some matters at Gravesend I was invited thither by water and carried aboard a New Englandman to drink strong waters. I was left sitting upon a chest below decks blessing myself for the company, but in no way dreaming I was to be part of the adventure or to be concerned in their voyage, when a boatswain came to me and asked me what provision I had aboard and where I would bestow myself? I replied that I could give him no account, and I called to the rest of my company. Then the whole crew of these cannibals fell into a passion of laughter. I began to think how I could escape, but was presently prevented and put into the hold where I found some others in like insensible condition. I was thus forced to wait till the Captain came on board when I was allowed on deck to present myself before him. I told him of the injury done me and my friends and at last won him over and was put ashore.'

The curious dress Mary affected, a man's doublet and a woman's petticoat, which she declared was ' a fit covering wherein every man might see the true dimensions of her body,' at length got her into trouble and she was cited to appear before the Court of Arches to answer to a charge of wearing man's apparel. She was sentenced to stand and do penance at St. Paul's Cross during the Sunday morning's sermon, a penalty commonly imposed at the time on women of loose character. Before she did her penance she consumed three pints of sack to sustain her during the ordeal.

' I did not say what I thought when my penance was over,' she remarks, ' but this dealing with me was far from reclaiming me to the sobriety of decent apparel, for I could by no means endure at any time the finical and modish excesses of attire in which women were then as in all ages very curious. . . . There was a neighbour of mine who being one time in her bravery, her husband liking and not liking the riches and grandery of her clothes, said to her : '' Sweetheart, you are very fine, but you never think of the charge ; there was never a time I have anything to do with you, but it stands me a crown towards this superfluity. '' Husband,'' said the dame, '' it is your own fault you pay so dear, for if you would do it oftener it would not be above a groat at a time, for I would rather take my money in such guise and parcels than in sums and in gross, provided the coin be current and not counterfeit.'' '

Mary, strangely enough, had a contemporary who was of a like hermaphrodite type and was known as ' Aniseed-water Robin.' Like her, he clothed himself partly in a man's and partly in a woman's dress. The boys in the street used to call him 'Moll's husband,' but she says, 'I had a natural abhorence to him.'

She tells us of a friend called Banks, a vintner, who had a favourite horse which he taught to dance and was so proud of him he shod him with silver shoes. One day he bet Mary twenty pounds that she would not ride from Charing Cross to Shoreditch astride a horse, in breeches and doublet, boots and spurs, like a man.

Mary says : ' I accepted his wager, and to do something more than my bargain, I got a trumpet and banner and threw it behind my back as trumpeters wear it. I proceeded in this way as far as Bishopsgate, where passing under the gate a plaguey orange-wench who knew me cried out : " Moll Cutpurse on horseback ! " All the folks ran out of their shops like mad, adding their cries : " Come down thou shame of women or we will pull thee down ! " I knew not what to do, but remembering a friend I had who kept a little victualing house a little further on, I spurred my horse on and reached the place, followed by the rabble who never ceased cursing me.

' In my own thoughts I was quite another thing. Methought, about the door were the very people who had gazed at Jane Shore in her scornful and unpitied misery, when she laid herself down to die in one of the adjacent ditches. In the undeserved lamentable fate of that noble dame and the penance she formerly underwent, I was something like her.

' By chance then a great wedding-party came by on foot and five or six bailiffs had arrested a man, whom the rabble turned to rescue. They forgot me, and getting out at the back of the houses I rode clear for Newington where I rested myself, and returning to Shoreditch later won my wager.'

Mary was a loyal supporter of the Monarchy, and

when the King returned to London in 1638, she describes how she greeted him : ' I resolved to show my loyal and dutiful respects to His Majesty and therefore undertook to supply Fleet Street Conduit, adjacent to my house, with wine to run continually on that triumphal day, which I performed with no less expense and the satisfaction of all comers.

' As the King passed by me, I put out my hand and caught him by his and grasped it very hard, saying : " Welcome home, Charles ! " His Majesty smiled. I believe he took me for some mad, bold Beatrice or other, while the people shouted and made a noise. This action of mine being the town-talk made people look on me at another rate than formerly. 'Twas no more " Moll Cutpurse," but " Mrs. Mary Thrift." '

Mary declares that she was the first woman in London to smoke, which in her time ' had only begun to be a great mode.' She says : ' I was mightily taken with this vanity and no woman before me ever smoked though many made to follow my example. . . .

' One time, a knave at a grocer's shop where I used to sit, at my demand of a pipe of smoke, presented me with a pipe full of gunpowder crowned at the top with tobacco, which little suspecting I took, when suddenly it fired in my mouth with such a blast and stench, belching and throwing out the ashes, that it was a little resemblance to Mount Etna. Perceiving it was but a boy's roguery, I restrained my passion further, then flung my pipe at his head.'

This strange character had a great love for dogs, which she kept in her house and taught all kinds of tricks. One dog she specially trained and it used to accompany her on her expeditions. She says : ' I had nine of a most lovely sort who were trimmed and looked to with the same care as other folks did their children. I always laid them in trundle beds with sheets and blankets, and was choice in their diet, boiling as the gentle do for their hunting dogs, a pot on purpose for them, with broth and meat, and they well show their breeding and education.'

' Moll ' was the heroine of the comedy, *The Roaring Girle,* written by Middleton and Dekker in 1611, and she was introduced by Field into his play *Amends for Ladies* in 1618.

As she grew older she gave up her evil ways and lived on her former gains until at length she was taken ill with dropsy, which she says, ' had such terrible symptoms I thought I was possessed and the devil had got into my doublet. I was forced to leave off that upper part of my garment and do penance again in a blanket, a habit distant from the Irish rug and Scotch plaid, the natural vests for women of quality, which my scoffing neighbours said I did very much resemble. I cannot further anatomize my body, for I dared not look at my legs, they did so represent a bull's or bear's stake and my head so wrapt up in cloaths that I looked like Mother Shipton.

' I will not boast of my conversion least I encourage other vile people to persist in their sins to the last, but I dare assure the world, I never lived a happy minute in it till I was leaving of it, and so I bid it adieu this three score and fourteenth year of my age.'

So died this strange creature at her house in Fleet Street, at the age of seventy-four. She was buried in the church of St. Bridget's. She had a remarkable dual character in which the feminine side appears to have predominated.

As customary at the time, someone wrote her epitaph, from which the following is an extract :

' Here lies under this same marble,
  Dust, for Time's last sieve to garble ;
  Dust to perplex a Sadducee
  Whether it rise a HE or SHE,
  Or two in one, a simple pair
  Nature's sport and now her care ;

For how she'll cloathe it at last day
(Unless she sighs it all away)
Or where she'll place it none can tell :
Some middle place 'twixt Heaven and Hell.'

Another wag composed an acrostic on her name
which ran :

' M erry I liv'd and many pranks I played,
A nd without sorrow now in grave am laid.
R est and the Sleep of Death doth now sure ease
Y outh's active sins and their old ag'd increase.

F amous I was for all the Thieving Art,
R enowned for what old woman ride in cart ;
I n pocket and in Placket I had part.
T his life I lived in Man's disguise :
H e best laments me that with laughter cries.'

T HE story of Catalina de Erauso, the Spanish nun who became famous as a soldier and fought with great courage in the wars in Chili and Peru in the seventeenth century, has been a theme of inspiration for several writers. De Quincey described her adventurous career ; it was dramatized in Spain, and her interesting story was told in Spanish verse by Jose Maria de Heredia in ' La nonne alferez,' and translated into French in 1894.

She had the distinction of being promoted to the rank of ensign on the field and was the first woman to be granted permission by a Pope to wear masculine attire.

She is said to have been born in San Sebastian in 1592, her father being Captain don Miguel de Erauso and her mother Dona Maria Perez de Galarraga y Arce. At an early age she was sent to a convent of Dominican nuns to be educated. She had three brothers in the service of the State, Miguel, the eldest, being an officer in the Army. After serving a year as a novice she was received into the community under the name of Catalina de Aliri. Later she fled from the convent, and, dressing herself as a man, she set off on her adventures. After serving as a page to Don Carlos de Arellano, a gallant soldier, she eventually made her way to Seville and enlisted in one of the galleons bound for the Spanish Main. On landing she joined the army under the name of Alonso Diaz Ramérez de Guzman and served through the campaigns against the Indians in Chili and Peru. She was under the command of Diego Brabo de Sarabía for over two years and afterwards was attached to the company of Captain Gonzalo Rodríguez, on whose recommendation she was promoted to the rank of ensign for distinguished service on the field.

She next served under Captain Guillén de Casanova, who commanded the garrison holding the fortress of Araoco, and was wounded at the battle of Purén. During the whole period of her service in Chile and Peru she preserved the secret of her sex and her disguise was never penetrated, not even by her brother, Ensign Miguel de Erauso, with whom she served unrecognized. In action she was conspicuous for her courage and daring, while her gambling propensities involved her in many brawls and fights. In one of these, when she was severely wounded and lay in a serious condition, she disclosed the secret of her sex to the Bishop of Guamanga. This ended her career as a soldier, and under the name of Antonio de Erauso she returned to Europe in 1624. Such briefly is her story.

According to the narrative of her life written by herself, Catalina made up her mind to leave the convent after a quarrel and conflict with ' a brawny nun who laid violent hands ' on her. This she deeply resented, and she determined to escape from the community ; while the nuns were rising from the midnight mass she managed to get hold of the convent keys and shut the doors of the building for the last time. She had made no special plans as to the route she should take, so she took shelter in a grove of chestnut trees outside the town to consider what she should do next. The first thing was to disguise herself, and she decided to dress in men's clothes in order to escape recognition. She cut out and made herself a pair of breeches from a blue cloth skirt she was wearing and from her linsey petticoat she fashioned a doublet and garters. She then cut off her hair and, arraying herself in the male garments she had made, set out on the third night, skirting the villages and keeping to the roads. She at length reached Vitoria, having eaten nothing but the herbs she found by the wayside. At Vitoria she sought refuge with a doctor named Don Francisade Cerralta, a professor who had married a first cousin of her mother's. He treated her with kindness and gave her clothes, and during the three months she stayed with him he taught her Latin. When she made up her mind to leave him she borrowed some money from the doctor, obtained a lift in a carrier's cart, and went to Valladolid, where she soon obtained employment as a page. While there she heard that her father had come in search of her, but she did not see him, so quickly packing up her things and with but eight doubloons in her pocket she set out for Bilbao. Later she went on to Estelle where she got work as a page again, but soon left for Pasage, where she boarded a ship sailing for Seville. There she enlisted as a boy on a galleon that formed part of the armada which had been fitted out for Punta de Araya, and sailed for America.

Landing at Panama she left the ship and took service with Captain Juan de Ibarra, Controller of the Treasury, and remained with him for three months.

Then Catalina's restless spirit asserted itself again ; she met with a merchant of Trujillo called Juan de Urquiza, and sailed with him in a frigate bound for Paita. There for a while she took charge of a shop for him, but in a brawl in which she was engaged she killed a man and afterwards fled to Lima. Now, having determined that fighting was her forte, she enlisted as a private in one of the six companies recruited for service in Chile, to form an army of 1600 men.

Arrived at Concepción she came across her brother, whom she had never seen, as he had gone to America before she was born. When he heard she had come from his native province in Spain he became greatly interested in her and got her transferred to his company. She served under him for three years without disclosing her identity.

At Concepción she led the rollicking life of a soldier, and later marched out with the army to the plains of Valdivia to engage the Indians who had massed there, and inflicted severe losses on the Spaniards. In one battle they attacked the ensign and captured the flag. Although wounded in the leg Catalina pursued them and with great bravery recaptured the flag and brought it back to the company. The Governor presented her with the flag she had saved and she was promoted to ensign in Alonso de Moreno's company.

Catalina served as an ensign for five years and was present at the battle of Purén, where her captain was killed and the company put under her command. She led it for six months, during which period they had many encounters with the Indians, and she received several arrow wounds. In one engagement she found herself in combat with a powerful Indian chief and un-horsed him in the fight ; he surrendered, but Catalina lost her temper, and had him hanged from a tree. Through this action she got into trouble with the Governor, who ordered her back to Nacimiento.

Now in disgrace, she was involved in several quarrels, and then set out for Tucuman on foot. At length, nearly exhausted by fatigue and hunger, she was given shelter at the house of a wealthy Indo-Spanish woman who treated her with great kindness and asked her to remain on and manage her household. This woman took a great liking to Catalina, and even wished her to marry her daughter, but she describes her as being ' very black and as ugly as the devil.' Catalina postponed the marriage under various pretexts until it became impossible for her to stay any longer, so she fled from her benefactor and the farm and went to Piscobamba. She stayed the night at the house of a friend, and after supper one evening joined in a gambling game with a Portuguese who was a great ruffian. Catalina won, but a quarrel arose and she dashed her cards in her opponent's face. They both drew their rapiers, but the onlookers intervened and held them back, and eventually the Portuguese paid up his losses and calm was restored.

' Three nights later,' says Catalina, ' at about eleven o'clock, when I was going home, I noticed a man standing at a street corner. I swung my cloak over my left shoulder, drew my rapier and went towards him. As I approached, he dashed at me, thrusting and calling out : " Cuckold ! Rascal ! " I knew his voice and ran my point into him and he fell dead. I then went to my friend's house, held my tongue and got into bed.

' Early next morning the Corregidor Don Pedro de Meneses came, roused me and walked me off. I reached the jail and was put in irons. About an hour after the Corregidor came with a notary and took my statement. I denied all knowledge of the business. Then they tortured me but I denied everything. When the case came on, witnesses I had never seen were produced and sentence of death was passed on me. I appealed, but an order to execute was issued. A monk came to hear my confession. I refused, and a cataract of monks was let loose on me.

' I was rigged out in a taffeta suit and hoisted on to a horse. They took me down unfrequented streets until we came to the gibbet. They placed the rope round my neck—but at this moment a messenger galloped in from La Plata. He was sent by the Secretary under orders from the President Don Diego de Portugal, and had an order to suspend my execution and transfer me to the High Court, twelve leagues away. The reason for this was extraordinary and a manifest mercy of God.

' I was sent under escort to La Plata and in twenty-four days was released.'

After this narrow escape Catalina set out again for Lima, where the Dutch were attacking the city with eight men-of-war. There she joined one of the five ships sent out from Callao to fight them.

' In the engagement,' she says, ' they hammered our flagship so heavily that she sank and not more than three contrived to escape by swimming. The three were myself, a barefooted Franciscan monk, and a soldier. All the rest perished.'

At Cuzco, later, Catalina again became embroiled in a fight in a gambling den and in the fray killed a notorious man called ' the Cid.' She was severely wounded, being stabbed in the left shoulder and deeply cut in the thigh. She was carried to her house and put to bed. A monk was called and she made her confession as she was afraid she was going to die. After she had received the Holy Viaticum she began to get better and gradually recovered, after being ill for four months.

A friend now came to her assistance and gave her a thousand pesos, three negroes and a mule, and thus accompanied she took the road to Guamanga. When she came to the bridge of Apurimac she was stopped by a constable who said : " You are arrested." Eight other constables came up and endeavoured to seize her, but Catalina resisted, drew her rapier and attacked them with vigour. During the fierce contest one of her negroes was killed and the constables, having lost three of their number, retreated, and Catalina proceeded on her way without further molestation.

On arriving at Guamanga she put up at an inn where she stayed for a time. Soon she began to frequent the gambling houses again, and one day when she was playing the Corregidor came into the room. He looked hard at Catalina and asked her where she had come from. She replied : " From Cuzco." He paused for a moment, then laid his hand on her, saying : " I arrest you." Catalina jumped up and her rapier flashed out as she got between him and the door. He called for help, but there was such a rush to the door that she could not get out, so she drew her pistol. A way was made for her and she ran off as fast as she could.

She lay low for a few days and then thought it would be better to change her lodging. She left the inn at nightfall, but had not gone far when she was challenged by two men. They tried to seize her, but she drew her rapier and on hearing the men call out : " Help in the name of the law ! " a crowd gathered and there was a great uproar. The Corregidor came out of the Bishop's house with several constables and called on his men to seize her. Catalina drew her pistol, fired and shot one of them, but at that point the Bishop, accompanied by four torch-bearers, came out and pushed their way into the middle of the crowd. As he reached Catalina he called out : " Ensign, give me your arms."

" I am surrounded by enemies, my Lord," she replied.

" Give them up," he cried. " You are out of harm's way with me and I pledge my word to see you safe out of this whatever it costs me."

" Most Illustrious Lord," Catalina answered, " when we reach the cathedral I will kiss your Lordship's feet."

' At this,' she continued, ' four of the Corregidor's slaves took hold of me and I had to use my hands to floor one of them. The Bishop caught me by the arms, took my weapons from me and led me along to his house. He had my wound attended to, gave me supper and a bed, then gave orders for me to be locked in.

' Next morning about ten o'clock, his lordship had

me brought into his presence and asked me who I was, where I came from, and all about my life. Seeing the saintly man he was and feeling that I was in the presence of God, I said to him : " My Lord, the truth is *I am a woman.*" Then I gave him an account of my life.

'While my story lasted, the Bishop sat in amazement, and when I had finished shed scalding tears. He then sent me to rest. Next morning he was convinced on the evidence of two matrons that I was a maid entire. His lordship embraced me tenderly, and later placed me in the convent of St. Clare at Guamanga.'

On the death of the Bishop, Catalina left the town for Lima. She was carried in a litter accompanied by six priests, four nuns, and six armed men. When they arrived she was taken to the Palace to see the Viceroy and later continued her journey to Santa Fé de Bogota. Everywhere the people thronged to catch a glimpse of the now famous 'Nun Ensign' whose story had been spread abroad.

She embarked for Spain and arrived at Cadiz on 1 November 1624. When she landed she was still wearing her military uniform, and aroused great interest wherever she went. Having been granted a pension by the King she set off on a pilgrimage to Rome. Her journey was an eventful one and she was arrested at one place and accused of being a Spanish spy. She was robbed of her money, her clothes were taken away, and she was put into irons for a fortnight. When she was liberated she resumed her journey and reached Rome on 5 June 1626. She is described at that time as being 'tall and burly for a woman, artificially flat-chested, not plain in feature and yet not beautiful, showing signs of hardship rather than of age. Her black hair was cut like a man's and hung in a mane as was customary at the time. She dressed in

Spanish fashion, wore a sword tightly belted, her head inclined forward and her shoulders slightly stooped, more like a fiery soldier than a courtier. She gesticulated with her plump, fleshy but massive and powerful hands, in a manner vaguely suggestive of her sex.'

She was lionized in Rome and Pope Urban VIII granted her special permission to continue to wear men's clothes and thus attired her portrait was painted by Francesco Crescentis. After staying about six weeks in Rome she went to Naples in July 1626. ' One day when sauntering on the quay,' she says, ' my attention was drawn to the guffaws of two wenches who were gossiping with a couple of youngsters and staring at me. I looked at them and one of them said : " Whither away my Lady Catalina ? " I replied : " To give you a hundred thumps on the scruff of your necks my lady strumpets, and a hundred slashes to anyone who defends you ! " They were silent and slunk off.'

At length, tiring of the monotony of city life, Catalina resolved to go abroad again, and she sailed for America in 1630. After her arrival she commenced business as a carrier and owned a number of negroes and mules.

Nicolas de Renteria, who saw her at Vera Cruz in 1645, says : ' She was regarded as a person of great courage and skilled in the use of arms. She dressed as a man and wore a rapier and dagger with silver mountings. She then looked about fifty years of age and was of good stature and stoutish build, with a dark complexion and a few hairs representing a moustache.'

While returning to Vera Cruz after a journey, she was taken ill at Cuitlaxtla, where she died in 1650. All the notables of the district came to her funeral, and she was buried with great pomp by the Church, for the story of Catalina de Erauso who had fought so bravely for her country had not been forgotten.

MORE than one Frenchwoman has emulated Joan of Arc in becoming a soldier and fighting for her country, and among these must be counted Christina, daughter of the Baron de Meyrac, of Bearn. The story of her life and adventures over two hundred years ago, if not entirely veracious, is one of romantic interest. She was idolized by her parents, and having been brought up in the country was devoted to all kinds of sport. At an early age she is said to have developed remarkable skill with the gun, and by the time she reached the age of nine she could handle and use all kinds of firearms. She could not be persuaded to look at a book or even to learn to read, and her parents, seeing it was useless to coerce her, allowed her to go hunting twice a week and gave her money to buy sufficient ammunition for her sporting excursions.

One day when out as usual for sport, she took a shot at some wild pigeons in a barn full of corn. It set fire to the building, which with its contents, was almost entirely destroyed.

Her father was very angry on hearing of this and refused to see Christina for several days, but at last he consented to forgive her if she promised never to handle a gun again. She felt the prohibition so greatly that her health was affected and her mother became anxious for her and persuaded the Baron to modify his command. Her gun was taken to the house of a neighbour and Christina, by her mother's permission, was occasionally allowed to go and use it.

Some time later she was invited with others to a

boar hunt and her brother formed one of the party. By some mischance she accidentally shot him and, seeing him fall, mad with grief, she fled in consternation into the country and was afraid to return home.

She ran and walked until she was almost exhausted and, at length, found herself near a castle where Abbé Dizesté, who was a relative of her family, lived. He listened to her story and at once rode off to ascertain if it was true and if the brother's wound had proved mortal. He found that it was only too true and that the young man had died on being carried back to his home. His father, the Baron, was distraught with grief and rage, and had gone searching for Christina with a pistol in his hand. The Abbé, seeing he could do no good, returned to the castle and informed Christina of her brother's death and her father's oath of vengeance. He resolved to keep her with him to prevent further trouble, and after consultation with other relatives, decided to send her to Spain and placed her in charge of his brother, who lived at Saragossa.

Christina, who was at this time about sixteen years old, had developed into a tall, fine, and handsome girl, and the Abbé began to have doubts as to the advisability of sending her to a strange country where he foresaw her beauty would soon attract attention. She had the lithe and well-knit figure of a boy, and all her inclinations were towards the pursuits followed by the male sex, such as hunting, riding, and fencing. He told Christina of the risks she would run as a girl in Spain, and she at once suggested that she should assume a boy's clothes, style, and manner, and in a foreign country no one would suspect the deception.

The Abbé at first thought the suggestion absurd and childish, but Christina declared that only so would her safety be ensured, and at length he agreed. Clothes suitable for a youth were obtained which became Christina well and thus transformed her into a good-looking boy, and so together they set out for Spain.

On arriving in Saragossa, the Abbé sought his brother, Don Lorenzo, and introduced Christina to him as a young kinsman who wanted to learn Spanish and study at the university.

Don Lorenzo agreed to give the 'young man' lodging and to watch over his training, and so the Abbé left the city, leaving Christina in his brother's charge.

The students at the university at that time wore long, loose black cassocks, and when Christina donned hers it made her look taller and even more like a young man than before, especially after she had had her light brown hair cut short after the Spanish fashion. Her appearance soon attracted the attention of her fellow-students, who called her the 'Handsome Frenchman,' and she became very popular with everyone. The students vied one with another for her friendship, and the young Marquess d'Osseyra used to call for her every morning in his coach to take her to lectures and Don Philip de Palasox, a son of the Marquesa d'Arizza, insisted on driving her back after the class was over.

Like the others, Christina carried a sword under her gown, and one evening when walking in the street with d'Osseyra they were attacked by a band of young ruffians who assailed them with insults and abuse. Christina and her friend drew their swords to defend themselves, but in the affray she received a wound in the stomach from a dagger, after which the assailants took to their heels.

D'Osseyra got help and had her carried to his house, where his mother at once sent for a surgeon. Christina would not allow him to examine the wound, as she knew it would be impossible to conceal her sex any longer, but as it continued to bleed profusely she asked to see the Marquesa alone and to her imparted her secret. The surgeon was bound to secrecy and he undertook to get the wound well in a week. The Marquesa was anxious to get Christina away and matters became more complicated when Don Lorenzo came and asked to see the wound in case it might be a mortal one. He also had to be told that his charge was a girl and not a boy, and on conferring with the Marquesa they agreed that it would be best for Christina as soon as she was well, in future to wear the clothes of a woman.

When she got better she returned to Don Lorenzo's house where her presence proved somewhat embarrassing, and he decided to place Christina in a nunnery for a time. Being acquainted with the Lady Abbess of the Ursulines, he approached her and the Abbess consented to receive Christina as a pensioner in the convent. There she soon gained the affection of the nuns, and her wit and good humour made her a favourite with all.

She had been at the convent for about six months when it was made known that the Archbishop of Saragossa was coming to pay a visit. In order to entertain him the pensioners were allowed to get up a little play in which Christina was cast for a leading male part.

Now the prelate, who had seen Christina several times as a student at the University, remembered her striking beauty and recognized her.

The play ended and the good nuns, expecting to receive applause and commendation, were astonished to see an expression of anger on the indignant Archbishop's face. He called the Lady Superior before him and demanded to know why she had introduced a young man into the convent. The Superior looked at him in amazement and declared that there was no man among the actors and that the play had been acted entirely by nuns who had long been in the house.

The Prelate then asked : " Who was it that played the part of Don Sancto Abarcas ? "

" It was a French maid-pensioner who has been well recommended," replied the Superior.

" You have taken a wolf and locked him up with the sheep," declared the Prelate sternly.

The Superior was astounded and said that the offending pensioner should be dealt with at once, but the Prelate, foreseeing a scandal, told her it would be best to keep a watch on the person in question and then to get rid of him as soon as possible.

Christina was greatly troubled when she heard of this. She knew that Don Lorenzo did not want her, so she at last appealed to the Marquesa d'Osseyra, who knew her secret, and obtained an invitation to stay at her house. Here she was again brought in contact with the young Marquess who had been her friend at the University, and it was not long before he fell deeply in love with her. He declared his passion and asked Christina to marry him, but she was not then prepared to accept his proposal and told him to wait ; if he was of the same mind in two years time she might consent.

Shortly afterwards news came of the death of Christina's father at Bearn, and of her mother's great desire to see her again. She bade farewell to the Marquesa and her son and set out for her home in France, where she received a warm welcome on her arrival.

For a short time she settled down with her mother in the country, and the young men in the district soon flocked to the château, where she was a great attraction. She had many offers of marriage, but always refused to surrender her liberty and sent all her suitors away disconsolate. Among them was the Vicomte Ronceval, who fought a duel over her with another admirer named Marmon. The Vicomte was fatally wounded by his adversary and Marmon fled to Paris, where through the influence of two of his friends he joined a company of the King's Musketeers.

After some time had elapsed he paid a visit to Bearn, and meeting Christina, told her of the great life he had had since he joined the Army under King Louis. This so worked on her imagination that she determined once more to play the part of a man and do service to the King. Leaving her affairs in the hands of her old benefactor, the Abbé Dizesté, she again assumed male attire, had her hair cut short, and with a foot-boy as attendant, set out for Paris.

She travelled under the name of St. Aubin and eventually arrived safely at her destination. Here she sought out a Chevalier Fourbon, an old friend who had considerable influence in high quarters, and on his recommendation she was nominated to the first company of the King's Guard. After going through a period of instruction in military exercises and training, St. Aubin became proficient in all his duties, and later, when the King came to inspect a general muster of his guards, he stood among the new musketeers in the ranks. He soon became very popular with his comrades, who declared St. Aubin was an Englishman. Christina did not contradict them, but allowed them to think she was a nephew of Lord Douglas.

After some time the musketeers were ordered to accompany the King to Flanders, where he was to join the Army then besieging Limbourg. The enemy, fearing the approach of the French, retired, giving out they were going to besiege Maestricht. The King then ordered a detachment of his musketeers under the command of M. Jauvelle to follow up and harass them, and St. Aubin was among this company. In one town he was billeted in the house of a wealthy burgher who had a wife and a sister who were considered great beauties. They received St. Aubin with delight and gave him the best room in the house and treated him like a prince.

He had not been there more than two days when it was evident that both the women had fallen passionately in love with him, to his great embarrassment. They showered gifts upon him, including a valuable locket encrusted with diamonds, and matters were approaching a crisis when the news came that the commander of the musketeers had received orders from the King to march to Paris. On their return to Paris St. Aubin was quartered at the Hôtel de Nôtre Dame, and there he came across another old friend in the person of the Baron de Quincy.

He was not long in Paris, however, for the King's Army was ordered once more to set out to besiege Condé. The campaign opened, and three days afterwards the musketeers were commanded to take a battery, and they behaved so gallantly that they not only put the enemy to flight, but also took the town by assault. St. Aubin showed great bravery during the action, and received a wound in the arm. Meanwhile, the Baron de Quincy had been commanded by the King to raise a regiment of horse at Tournai, and, meeting St. Aubin at the house of the Governor, he offered him the command of a company in the new regiment, which he accepted. With this company he made many raids on the enemy's lines and showed the greatest courage and bravery. In one engagement he was again wounded rather seriously and was ill for some time. As a result he resolved to return to France and give up the Army.

So St. Aubin left Brussels, where he had been staying, and took a passage in a ship for Spain. The captain of the ship in which he sailed had heard fabulous stories of his exploits during the war, and later, when he landed at a Spanish port and travelled to Madrid, St. Aubin found there were reports about that his bravery was due to supernatural powers. Don Juan of Austria, however, to whom he was known, assured him that he would be well treated and should have board and lodging at the King's expense.

After regaining her health and living unmolested in Madrid, news came to Christina one day of the taking of St. Gistain by the French. This greatly alarmed and excited the Spanish, who vented their rage on all the French people then living in the country.

They sacked their shops, seized their goods, and banished them from the towns. Christina did what she could to help and assist her countrymen and through her influence with Don Juan the persecution was lessened, but her interference was much resented by the people. The report was again spread about that she was a witch, for how else, they asked, could a French woman influence the Governor? At length the Inquisition took notice of these rumours and Christina was arrested.

A fortnight elapsed before she was questioned, and by that time fresh stories had been gathered of her adventures with the Army in the Low Countries. It was said that she had bewitched some of the generals, and other absurd charges were brought against her. It was declared that it was by witchcraft that she had unhorsed a certain Count Talera when she was only carrying a cane.

She was asked what made her disguise herself like a man, and she replied that from her childhood she had had a strong inclination for arms and that her parents had allowed her to wear boy's clothes. By a strange coincidence the Archbishop of Saragossa, who had remembered her as a student at the University and had exposed her at the convent, was one of the Inquisitors ; through him she obtained her freedom.

After this she was more than ever resolved to carry out her intention of entering a convent and taking the veil, but she changed her plans when her old admirer, the Marquess d'Osseyra, sought her out and begged her to marry him. Although she liked him she still refused his offer, and, determined now to leave Spain, she again assumed male attire.

She had a great desire to see England, and finding the British envoy was about to leave Madrid to return to his country she managed to get engaged as a foot-boy to a member of his entourage. After she arrived in London she was suddenly taken ill, but was well treated and gradually recovered her health. She had made several friends, among them two young English-men who greatly desired to see foreign service. When the news arrived in London that the King of France had opened a campaign for the conquest of Ghent, Christina and her two English friends crossed the Channel and joined the French Army.

At the siege of Yprès she was again seriously wounded by a musket-ball and was carried to Brussels. She was taken to a hospital, where fever set in and her life was despaired of. When asked if she had any friends she would like to see, she begged the Lady Superior of the hospital to send for the Marquess d'Osseyra, who she knew was at Bruges. He came at once to her bedside, and although she was too weak to speak she recognized him. She stretched out her arm and clasped his hand, and, comforted by the man who loved her, Christina died after a life full of strange adventures.

SOME two hundred years ago, when travellers had to brave the dangers of the road on horseback or by coach, they never knew when they might not be stopped and asked to hand over their money and valuables, to an individual mounted and masked, who pointed a pistol at their heads. Many romantic stories are told of these ' knights of the road,' some of whom were young men of good families, like the young Verneys of Tring, who adopted this easy method of lining their depleted pockets.

Tom Rowland, it is said, used to dress as a woman on some of his expeditions and gracefully collected the jewellery reluctantly handed over to him by his victims. At times Jack Shepherd also masqueraded in female costume when he waylaid travellers on Hounslow Heath. He escaped from Newgate in 1724 dressed in women's clothes which had been smuggled into the prison, slipped past the lodge where the turnkeys were carousing, and so regained his freedom.

It was rarely, however, that a woman played the part of highwayman, but there is a story concerning the beautiful Lady Maude Ferrars which tells how she ' took to the road ' on more than one occasion and eventually paid the penalty with her life. Although now legendary, the story long survived in the district of Hertfordshire where she lived.

Away on the Great North Road between St. Albans and Dunstable there once stood an old house in a beautifully wooded park, the home of Sir John Ferrars. When he died at the end of the seventeenth century there was no male heir, and it later passed to his granddaughter Maude, a spirited young girl who gave promise of developing into a woman of great beauty. After the Restoration the estate was impoverished and very little money was left to Maude to keep it up, but she determined to make a struggle to do so.

When she was scarcely fourteen it had been arranged that she should marry young Viscount Fanshawe, an Irish peer, and he was but sixteen when the marriage took place. Very soon afterwards he left his young bride to return to his home in Ireland, and she was left alone in the house of her ancestors.

When she reached the age of twenty Maude had grown into a beautiful and vivacious girl, full of life and vitality. Her dark hair, which she wore short, was a mass of curls, and this gave her a very boyish appearance. Her neighbours were scandalized when she decided to adopt male attire. She had a passion for horses and was rarely out of the saddle. Astride her favourite mare she rode like the wind and she was well known throughout the country-side. Naturally, Maude had many admirers among the young men of the district, in particular, young Lord Tanadale, a foppish youth who constantly sought her company and pestered her with his attentions.

She loved to ride wildly across the country at night, to the dismay of the villagers, some of whom declared that she once ' kicked off the top of the church steeple with her mare's hoofs.' Others swore they had seen her leap over the tops of the trees in the old rookery one night, like a witch, while the moon was shining bright.

Her youthful husband appears to have completely deserted her, and she was left to her own resources in the old house at Markyate, where her staff consisted of one ancient dame who had been with the family for years, and Roger Frost, who had served her grandfather as groom and now watched over Maude with fatherly care and devotion.

At length, her night rides became the talk of the neighbours, it was whispered at the ' Goat and Compasses ' that she had become a ' knight of the road.' Maude, however, only smiled when old Roger repeated the gossip he heard at the village inn. He knew how often she rode out on these wild escapades by the condition in which he found her mare Brown Bess in the morning. He would growl to dame Eliza : " Sweat, foam, and lather . . . laying down in her stall . . . sich a sight for a father ! Saddle and bridle as hung there kvite clean over night vas all mud and not fit to be seen. . . . Thrice a veek or fower times perhaps (more or less so to speak) l've diskivered that there identical mare or else the Black Barb, vich you'll remember was brought from o'er seas last September."

Annoyed by the repeated importunities of Lord Tanadale, who now often tried to waylay her on her night excursions, Maude determined to frighten him off by stopping him on the road.

One night, knowing he would be dining at a friend's house where his potations would be long and deep, and that he would be returning to his home in the early hours, no doubt, only just sober enough to sit his horse, she set out about midnight for the lane he had to traverse. The road dipped into a little vale, the bottom of which was bordered by some tall elms which gave excellent cover. Choosing a suitable spot where it was very dark under the trees, Maude backed her mare on to the grass by the roadside to await her quarry. She had timed it well, for before many minutes she heard the steady clip-clop of a horse coming down the hill towards her, and a raucous voice she knew well chanting : " Here's to the maid of charming sixteen."

She waited until he was within a few yards of her, then with a touch of the spur she suddenly brought her mare across the lane and presented a pistol at the young man's head and called out in as gruff a voice as she could command : " Ho, there ! Stand and deliver ! Your money or your life ! "

The young man pulled up sharply, but for some moments his fuddled brain did not take in what had happened.

" Throw down your purse and ride on," came the voice in peremptory tones once more.

Unable to see his assailant, and scared by the sight of the pistol, Lord Tanadale fumbled in his pocket and threw his purse to the ground with a curse, then, putting spurs to his horse, rode off without waiting to see what happened. He was followed by a merry ringing laugh and a voice singing : " Unlucky, un-lucky, my lord ! Give the highwayman's love to the fair Mistress Maude."

Now, at Markyate, there was a small door in the base of a turret at the side of the house of which Lady Maude alone had the key. It opened on to a secret staircase which communicated with the dressing-room where she was accustomed to change her costume and so get to her bed-chamber unknown to those in the house. So after stabling her mare she retired to rest, well pleased with her night's escapade.

The story of how Lord Tanadale was held up in Lone Lane soon got abroad, and lost nothing in the telling, for some declared that shots had been exchanged and that, although he had escaped, he had winged his assailant. The rumours that a notorious highwayman was operating in the district caused great disquietude, and the villagers began to be afraid to go out at night.

Maude, however, only smiled when she heard the gossip, and emboldened by her success determined to again try her prowess as a highwayman.

An opportunity occurred when Roger told her one day that Master Zachary Blair, the mayor, was going to St. Albans market to sell some cattle. Maude had a grudge against Blair, a vulgar and overbearing man whose ambition was to make a position in the neighbourhood and who had long tried to buy some of her land for a very low price. She thoroughly hated him and he was generally disliked, for it was believed he had gathered his wealth by questionable means ; in any case he was noted for sharp practice. She found out the day on which he was going to market, and made her plans accordingly. It was a cold and misty night when Blair, having sold fifteen head of cattle and a mare, left St. Albans and started to jog home on his nag. His way lay through a lonely lane that emerged on to a desolate common which he had to cross. His pocket was heavy with a bag of money, for he had done good business. He was wondering how soon he could put it safely in the bank when suddenly a horseman came up behind him and seized the bridle of his horse.

" Stop and deliver ! " a cry rang out, as a pistol was thrust in his face.

Blair was terrified, for he was quite unarmed, and he realized that shouting for help in that lonely spot was useless. Afraid for his life he pulled the heavy bag from his pocket and handed it over to his assailant without a word.

" Many thanks, good sir," muttered the masked figure, who promptly took it, and cleverly wheeling her horse galloped off across the common.

There was naturally much excitement when it was heard that no less a person than the mayor had been waylaid and robbed. Blair reported the matter to the Council, which was called together to consider what could be done. Although some laughed and jeered at his worship for handing over his money so tamely, it was resolved that steps must be taken to put a stop to highway robbery and the highwayman must be hunted down and captured.

A committee was formed consisting of Lord Tanadale, who was still very sore about his adventure,
Zachary Blair, his fellow-sufferer, Oxley the butcher,
Doughty the baker, and farmer Ducket, who was
famous as a huntsman. To strengthen the band it was
agreed to engage the services of Jonathan Blaker, a
well-known Bow Street runner, whom they thought
from his experience in thief-catching would be
invaluable.

Old Roger heard all this gossip at the ' Goat and
Compasses ' and brought back the news to his mistress,
who was much amused when she heard it, and at once
resolved with her usual impetuosity to give the hunters
a good run for their money. Telling Roger to find out
the nights they were going out on the hunt and the
way they were likely to go, she determined to hold up
the party. At length, hearing the committee men
were going to patrol a lonely road which led to a heath
locally known as ' No Man's Land,' she set out shortly
after midnight one Friday, mounted on Brown Bess, in
the direction of Harpenden.

Saving her mare, she rode very slowly until she
reached the first signpost, when she heard a shout from
a narrow lane close to where the band had been lying
concealed.

" That's him ! " called a loud voice which she recognized as Blair's. And the company emerged from the
lane at a gallop.

Maude, taken by surprise, spurred her mare forward
across the heath. She saw at once that she would be
outmatched by a band of mounted men and flight was
her only chance. The chase began. Brown Bess, on
her mettle, got well into her stride and was soon a good
distance ahead. Glancing over her shoulder Maude
saw her pursuers come to grief one by one, until at last
only one remained. She slackened rein for a moment.
Then a shot rang out which echoed in the night, and

Maude knew by a hot, searing pain that she had been hit in the back. Undaunted, she bent down over the mare's neck and spurred Brown Bess towards home. She quickly lost sight of her pursuer who proved to be Blaker, the Bow Street runner.

Now, faint and weak from the bullet wound, which she felt was bleeding profusely, she at length arrived at the door of Markyate and fell off the exhausted mare on the steps. There she lay unconscious, her life's blood ebbing away.

It was the neighing of Brown Bess that at length aroused old Roger, who, candle in hand, opened the door and saw his beloved mistress lying across the threshold. He raised her tenderly, but no word came from her, and with a wan smile on her pallid face she died in his arms.

Thus, according to the old story, the beautiful Maude Ferrars fell a victim to her masculine escapades, which indeed may be regarded as the mischievous pranks of a high-spirited girl rather than as actual highway robbery.

A MONG the women who posed as men and served as soldiers in the British Army in the early eighteenth century, none showed more courage and bravery than Christian Davies. The story of her career and adventures marks her as a woman of extraordinary determination and character, who faced the dangers of a soldier's life with the greatest equanimity.

She was born in Dublin in 1667, her father being a maltster and brewer in a good way of business in that city. Her parents gave her the best education possible at the time, and afterwards her lively and active disposition led her to help her mother with the work on a farm they rented. She loved country life and learned to follow the plough and thresh the corn ; she could turn her hand to any work as well as the best of the men on the land.

She was a good rider and often rode astride a favourite grey mare, jumping the hedges and ditches across the country-side. When in some districts the Irish rallied to the cause of James II, her father sold the corn on the farm and joined the Army in support of the King. The battle of the Boyne, however, put an end to his hopes for the cause, and after their defeat, in company with a Frenchman, he made his way home. His companion, who was known as Captain Bodeaux, fled with him to his house and was afterwards placed in command of troops at the siege of Limerick, where, while defending the bridge with great gallantry, he was killed. When they came to remove his uniform and clothes it was discovered that the Captain was a woman, an incident which probably left an impression on Christian's mind.

When the war was over she went to live with an aunt with whom she remained for four years, and on her death she was left heiress to all her aunt's property, including a well-furnished house. Here Christian, now provided with means, carried on with farming and kept a number of horses, her overseer being a young man called Richard Welsh, who had been in her aunt's employ. She describes him as 'handsome in appearance with a manly face, an open temper, sober and active in business, and a man any woman might love.'

It is little wonder, therefore, that Christian developed a strong affection for him. At first she thought it would be beneath her to think of marrying a man who was really her servant, but love overcame her resolutions, her pride vanished, and she awaited his declaration.

Although Richard adored Christian he was too bashful to broach the subject of love to his mistress and first sought the good offices and advice of a friend of hers. This friend told him that she was sure Christian wished to marry him and was only waiting to be asked. So Richard plucked up courage and acted on this advice ; finding Christian at her house he offered her his heart.

" Believe me, my dear mistress," he exclaimed, " I have no views of interest. I love you for yourself and not for your money. I will never pretend to be other than a just steward should you consent to make me the happiest of men."

Christian did not need much persuasion, and embracing him she replied that she had long been waiting for him to ask her, and consented. They were married within a week and settled down very happily in their new relationship. All went well with them for a few years, during which time Christian gave birth to two children.

One day Richard Welsh left the house in the morning

to pay an account of fifty pounds which was owing —and did not return. As day after day went by Christian became prostrate with grief and anxiety. She could not account for his sudden disappearance, his desertion of herself and the children, yet she could not believe he had met with his death.

At length she learned that he had paid the money owing and had then left in company with an unknown man. A year went by and Christian heard nothing more. She threw herself actively into the work of her farm, which, with the care of her children, occupied all her time.

After a further twelve months Christian received a letter from her missing husband. In explanation of his absence he declared that he had become completely intoxicated after drinking with a stranger in a tavern, and he knew nothing until he found himself on board a ship carrying recruits. By the time he had recovered from the effects of the drink, the ship had reached Helvoet Sluys, where he was put on shore without a penny in his pockets. He had tried in vain to find a ship to take him back home, and the ensign in charge of the recruits advised him to enlist in some regiment. As he was without money he was compelled to do this, and much against his will he joined up with a regiment of foot.

When Christian read this letter she was at first completely overcome and could not understand why Richard had been so long in communicating with her. She decided to go and find him and bring him back.

At first she had no idea how this was to be done ; then, probably recalling the incident of ' Captain Bodeaux ' and how she had succeeded in disguising herself as a man, Christian did not see why *she* should not conceal her sex and join the Army and go to Flanders. At length she made her plans and placed her children in the care of her mother and a nurse and her house and land with friends. She then cut her hair short and dressed herself in a suit of her husband's clothes ; she took the precaution of quilting the waist-coat and bought a wig, a hat, some Holland shirts, and a silver-hilted sword. She managed to conceal fifty guineas in the waistband of her breeches so that she could carry it without suspicion, and having thus completed her preparations she set out on her quest.

Riding to the town she disposed of her horse and made her way to the sign of the ' Golden Last,' where Ensign Herbert Lawrence kept his rendezvous for beating up recruits for the Army in Flanders.

She offered him her services to fight against France and show her zeal for King William. The Ensign, after declaring that she looked ' a clever, brisk young fellow,' gave her a guinea as enlisting money and a crown to drink the King's health. He ordered her to be en-rolled as ' Christopher Welsh ' in Captain Tichbourne's company of foot, in the regiment commanded by the Marquis de Pisare ; the lieutenant in charge of the company being called Gardner. After staying a short time in Dublin, Christian was shipped with other recruits to Holland, where they were landed at William-stadt and then marched to Gorkum. Next day they set out for Landen, where they were incorporated in various regiments.

Christian threw herself wholeheartedly into her training and soon became proficient in drill and mili-tary exercises ; she was even commended by the officers for her smartness and aptitude. Her regiment was now ready to join the Grand Army, which was in expectation of a general battle as they were now within cannon-shot of the enemy.

Shortly after she reached Landen Christian was ordered on the night-guard posted at the bedroom door of the Elector of Hanover. While she was there on duty, she tells us, ' Mustapha, a Turk and valet to His

Highness introduced to his master's room a fine, handsome, jolly lady, a black beauty dressed in rich silk and a bedgown tied with ribbons from her breast to her feet.' She goes on : ' I thought the lady went in with a great deal of alacrity. I believed many more of our sex would visit a sovereign prince with a particular satisfaction, especially if he was as agreeable in his person as the Elector, who then wore his own hair— the finest I ever saw.'

As the French Army drew nearer and the troops of the Allies engaged, Christian heard the shot rattle about her. It made her afraid at first, but she soon recovered her courage. She was ordered by Lord Cholmondeley to return to her regiment, and while she was trying to do so she received a wound in the leg from a musket-ball. Lord Cholmondeley, who saw her fall, ordered her to be carried off the field.

Christian was disabled for two months with the wound. By the time that she was fit for service again winter was approaching, and her regiment was ordered into quarters at Gertruydenberg.

The village was near the dikes, and while the regiment were there they began to give way. The English soldiers were ordered to assist the Dutch in repairing them, and the men were obliged to work night and day up to their waists in water. Christian, who, with Lieutenant Gardner, was busy in a trench, narrowly escaped drowning, for the tide rose rapidly, and they had to wade out hand in hand.

The following summer was spent in marches and countermarches, watching the movements of the French. One day, when Christian's detachment was engaged in foraging, the French suddenly attacked the party. Thus surprised, Christian and sixty of her comrades were taken prisoners, and after being robbed of their belongings they were taken by tedious marches to St. Germain-en-Laye.

On their arrival the Dutch and English soldiers were herded together, but on the following night, owing to the intervention of the English Queen, who was then at the Court of St. Germain, they were separated and given clean straw every night to sleep on. They were allowed five farthings each daily for tobacco, a pound of bread, and a pint of wine. The Duke of Berwick came to visit them to see that they were not ill-treated, and he advised them to take service with the French. When he thus spoke to Christian, she replied : " I have taken the oath to King William and I could not in honour break my engagement."

After they had been imprisoned for some nine days a Mr. Van Deden arrived to effect an exchange with some French prisoners, and Christian with her comrades was liberated.

' We went to the Palace,' she says, ' to return Her Majesty our grateful thanks. She consented to see us and told me I was " a very pretty young fellow " and that it grieved her much that I had not had my liberty sooner.

' On rejoining the army we heard the news of the death of Queen Mary in England, and soon afterwards we drew off again into winter quarters at Gorkum.'

While there Christian had an adventure which is best told in her own words. She says : ' I began to indulge my natural gaiety of temper and lived very merrily. In my frolic I made my addresses to a burgher's daughter who was young and pretty. I squeezed her hand whenever I could get an opportunity and sighed when in her company, I looked foolishly and practised upon her all the ridiculous airs which I had often laughed at. The poor girl grew really fond of me.

' When I was with her she always regaled me in the best manner possible—nothing was too good for me. It was true she did not scruple to own she loved me, but she avowed she loved her virtue better than her life.

' If I had dishonourable designs on her I was not the man she loved,' continues Christian. ' She told me that in the course of this affair a sergeant of the regiment had also fallen to her charms, but finding I was preferred he resolved to make a desperate assault on her virtue. One day when I was under arms, the sergeant came bravely to her and tried to obtain by force what he could not gain by assiduity. She defended herself stoutly but in the struggle which ensued she lost her cap and most of her clothes were torn off her back. Attracted by her cries, friends came to her assistance and the sergeant beat a retreat.

' No sooner had she recovered from his assault than she came in search of me, to find me in my rank, standing at arms. She told me what had passed and begged me to revenge the insult on her. When I was dismissed by my officer I went in quest of my rival and demanded to know how he had dared attempt the honour of a woman who, for aught he knew, was my wife ? I told him his conduct cast a reflection on the corps and required immediate satisfaction. He called me a proud insolent coxcomb.

' " I leave Billingsgate language to women," I replied. " If you have as much courage in the force of a man as you have in assaulting defenceless women, come with me at once to yonder windmill and I will soon convince you that General T—— had too good an opinion of you when he took his livery off your back to put on the King's and gave you a halberd."

' I knew the fellow had been footman to General T—— and this reproach stung him to the quick. He replied that he would soon cool my courage and we went off together to the windmill where we both drew and engaged.

' The first thrust I made gave him a slanting wound in his right breast which well nigh finished the business. He returned this with a long gash in my right arm, but before he could recover his guard I gave him a thrust in the right thigh about half a span from the " Pope's eye." The next pass he aimed at my breast, but it hit my right arm, though it was little more than a prick of a pin. He then grew weak with loss of the blood which now flowed plentifully from his wound.

' By this time some soldiers on duty had seen our first attack, and a file of musketeers under the command of a sergeant came up and took us prisoners, disarmed us both and sent him to hospital. As my wounds were slight and I was the aggressor and but a common soldier I was taken to prison, for the sergeant was thought to be mortally wounded and he did not recover for a long time.

' I sent my sweetheart an account of what had happened and where I was confined. She acquainted her father with the villainous attempt the sergeant had made upon her and let him know it was her quarrel which I had taken up. The father at once acted and made a proper representation of the affront offered to a member of his family, with the result that in four days' time I received a pardon from King William and an order for my immediate release. My sword was returned, my arrears paid, and I was given my discharge from the regiment.

' The moment I was released I went to thank my deliverer, and she gratefully acknowledged the risking of my life in revenging the insult done to her. In the end she made me a proposal of marriage.

' " My dear," I said, " you offer me the greatest happiness this world can afford me. Will you give me leave to ask your father ? "

' " My father ! " she cried. " You cannot imagine that a rich burgher will allow his daughter to marry a foot-soldier ? For though I think you merit everything, yet my father will not view you with my eyes."

' This answer was what I expected, for it was because I knew her father would refuse his consent that I had asked to speak to him.

' " What then can be done ? " I asked.

' " I will run the hazard of your fortune in case my father proves irreconcilable after our marriage," she replied. I told her there were two obstacles to that proposal and declared I must gain a commission or purchase one in order to deserve her.

' Thus I got off from this *amour* without loss of credit and was discharged from my regiment.

' I was uncertain what to do, but loath to leave the army. So I sought Lieutenant Keith and rejoined in Lord John Hayes' regiment of dragoons.

' We were soon ordered to the siege of Namur which King William had invested. He opened the trenches before the city in two different places and it capitulated on 4 August, but the French bombarded Brussels to save the citadel. This made the Allies redouble their efforts at Namur.

' Never was more terrible fire seen, for no less than sixty large battering pieces and as many mortars played incessantly on the outworks. Marshal Boufflers, seeing no likelihood of saving the citadel, retreated when most of the fortifications of Namur were demolished.

' Nevertheless we lost a thousand men in the assault on the new castle and while the King was preparing for a second attempt, Marshal Boufflers surrendered on terms, and the Allies took possession on the evening of 1 September.'

Christian continued in the same regiment of dragoons until the King reviewed the Army on the Plain of Breda, after which it was disbanded.

Her thoughts then turned to home. She knew not what might have happened in her absence, and to assure herself she set out for Dublin, which she reached in safety. She decided not to make herself known, so after ascertaining that her mother and children were well, she resolved to continue a soldier's life.

After all the vicissitudes and the adventures she had gone through Christian could not remain idle for long. On hearing that a new war was breaking out in Italy and that the Dutch were massing troops near Rosendaal, she again took ship for Holland. On arrival she sought out Lieutenant Keith, her previous commander, who was re-forming her old corps, and she at once re-enlisted in the dragoons under Lord John Hayes.

The first action in which the regiment engaged was at Ninmeguen, where they were roughly handled by the French. After this they took part in the siege of Kaisersweert, during which Christian formed one of a party of horse and dragoons detached from the main army for reconnaissance, under the command of General Domprè. They fell in with a superior force of French cavalry and put them on the run, but Christian escaped unwounded and afterwards took part in the sieges of Stevens, Weert, and Ruremond.

When the Army went into winter quarters Christian at length began to think of her husband, whom she had come to seek. She had made many inquiries in various places, but all had been in vain ; she concluded he must have been killed and that she had lost him for ever.

In March 1703 the Duke of Marlborough landed in Holland and took command of the Army to open a new campaign. On 24 April they invested Bonn, which capitulated in four days. Then came disaster for Christian, for at Donawert she received a ball in her hip which lodged between the bones and deprived her of the use of her thigh and leg. She was carried to a hospital near Schellenberg and received attention from three of the best army surgeons, Wilson, Laurence, and

Sea. While there, the secret of her sex, which she had managed to conceal successfully for so long, was nearly discovered ; but eventually she got her discharge with her secret still intact. On leaving the hospital, she was glad to receive her share of the plunder taken at Ulm and the cities in Bavaria, whither the Army had marched.

Christian was next engaged in the battle of Hochstet, and, although she was often in the thickest part of the fight, she escaped without a wound. Afterwards her troop was detached to guard the prisoners and march them to the plain of Breda. On the way, during a halt, while watching the women bewailing the loss of husbands and brothers who had fallen at Schellenberg and Hochstet, she noticed a woman talking to a man whose face seemed very familiar to her. She drew nearer to the palisade where her horse was tied and looking through saw the man turn to embrace the woman. She was struck with amazement when she recognized him as Richard Welsh, her missing husband. She was so surprised that she shook with emotion and for a moment was paralysed. After she had seen him embrace the Dutch woman, she resolved not to make herself known to him yet. She joined a comrade, who asked her what was troubling her (for she was trembling from head to foot), and told him she had just encountered her brother, Richard Welsh, whom she had not seen for twelve years.

She pointed out the man, who was in the uniform of Orkney's regiment, to her comrade and told him to find out if his name was Richard Welsh, and to ask when he had last heard from his wife. He went at once and she saw him speak to the soldier and receive a reply, but he had hardly returned when the drums and trumpets sounded to resume the march to Breda.

On arriving there, after housing the prisoners, Christian went in search of the soldier who she believed to be her husband, and on inquiring at the main-guard, was told he was in an ale-house nearby. She entered it and passed through an outer room to the kitchen, where she saw the man drinking with the Dutch woman. Taking a good look at him she was now sure that he was indeed her husband.

Christian then asked the landlady to show her to a private room ; she was no sooner there than she was convulsed with grief. She lay down and cried until her tears ceased ; then she bathed her face and calling the landlady ordered some beer to be brought. When the woman had brought it, she asked her to go and tell the soldier of Orkney's regiment who was drinking in her kitchen to come and speak to her.

' I sat with my back to the light,' says Christian, ' so that he might not see my face. Presently he came in and I saluted him by name, adding that I had the advantage, for I found I knew him although I appeared to be a stranger to him. " Sir," I said, " you are not unknown to me. Pray when did you hear from your wife and children ? "

' " Sir," he replied, " I have heard no news of them these twelve years though I have written no less than a dozen letters to her which I am apt to believe have miscarried."

' " There are many pretty girls here, no doubt, who served to compensate for her absence," I remarked.

' " Sir," he replied, " you take me for a villain and you lie."

' A sudden tremor seized me of which he who had his hand on his sword took notice, and looking in my face more intently he stepped forward crying : " Oh Heavens ! Is this possible ? Can I believe my eyes or is it a delusion. Do I really see my dear Christian ? " He clasped me in his arms, kissed me in rapture and bedewed my cheeks with tears of joy.

' As soon as I could disengage myself, I told him of

my search and all I had been through to find him and how I had left children and home to face the dangers of a soldier's life for his sake.

' " My dear Christian," he said, " do not embitter the joy of this meeting by cruel and undeserved reproaches. Had you received my letters you would have learnt of my misfortunes. It was not my fault. I gave you a true account."

' Meanwhile the Dutch woman, who had been waiting in the kitchen below, came upstairs, knocked at the door, and asked why he had left her so long alone ? '

Stirred by jealousy, Christian called to her : " Is this man your husband ? "

' " Yes," the woman replied.

' Richard denied it, but she declared they had lived together as man and wife.'

He bade her leave them, and after she had gone Christian told her husband that she liked her life in the Army so much that she was going to continue it. If he would pass as her brother and not claim her as his wife, and would promise not to reveal the secret of her sex, she would give him all that he wanted. To this arrangement he eventually agreed, and after giving him a piece of gold he took leave of her with a passionate embrace and they separated to their respective camps.

For a time they saw each other every day, like brothers, and their real relationship was kept secret.

The Dutch Army, at this time not being strong enough to keep the field, was entrenched under the guns of Maestricht, while the French left their lines and invested Huy, and after taking it laid siege to Liége. The Duke of Marlborough had no sooner arrived at Maestricht than the French abandoned Liége, raised the siege, and withdrew. At the battle of Ramillies, Christian was again in the hottest part of the fight, and escaped unhurt until the French were defeated, when a shell (fired from a steeple on which before the battle they had placed mortars and cannon) burst close to her and she was struck by a fragment, which fractured her skull. She was carried to Meldret, a small town near Louvain, and taken to hospital, where it was found necessary to trepan her and it was ten weeks before she recovered. For some days she had been unconscious and during that time the surgeons who were attending her discovered her true sex. They at once informed Brigadier Preston, who was in charge of the British, that his ' pretty dragoon ' (as Christian was usually called) was in fact *a woman*. He was loath to believe it, and on seeing Christian told her he had always looked upon her as ' the prettiest fellow and the best man he had.'

He sent for Richard Welsh and said : " I am surprised at a piece of news these gentlemen tell me. They say your brother is in reality a woman ! "

" Sir," said Richard, " since she is discovered I cannot deny it. She is my wife and I have had three children by her."

Christian's story soon spread throughout the camp, and among others who heard of it and came to see her, was Lord John Hayes. He asked her no questions, but spoke to a comrade who had formerly shared her tent, and he declared that he never knew or even suspected she was other than a man.

Lord John then called Richard and asked him to explain the meaning of the disguise. He gave full and satisfactory answers and told him how he had first met Christian and married her, also how they came to be separated.

Lord John was greatly interested in the story and ordered that Christian should want for nothing and her pay should be continued. He sent her a parcel of shirts and sheets to make clothes and Brigadier Preston made her a present of a handsome silk gown, while all the officers of the regiment contributed something to pay for dresses. Lord John also spoke to her about her treatment of Richard and now that her sex had been discovered he told her there was no longer any reason for disguise.

" My Lord," said Christian, " the discovery of my sex has now removed the cause and I have no objection to living with him as is the duty of an honest wife."

" Well," said Lord Hayes, " we will have a new marriage."

' All the officers of the regiment were invited,' says Christian, ' and we were wedded and bedded with great solemnity. The sack-posset was eaten, the stocking thrown and every one on leaving kissed the bride and left a piece of gold.'

Although she had resumed her married life, Christian could not remain idle for long, so she offered to undertake the cooking for the regiment, returning to her husband's quarters every night. After that she turned subtler and was allowed to pitch her tent at the front, while the others were driven to the rear of the Army.

Christian Davies records but little more of her army experiences, although we learn she served as a soldier on General Webb's expedition, when between Ostend and Ghent a convoy was attacked by the French. She followed her husband to Ghent, where she took a hand in some smuggling operations that were going on. Here she came in for more plunder and got ' a bay horse with silver-capped pistols and laced housings.' She also occupied herself in fishing up with a grappling-iron plate and copper which had been thrown down the wells.

One day, towards the close of Marlborough's campaign in the Low Countries, Christian was walking through a wood after an engagement when she came across a dog which led her to a wounded man. He proved to be her husband, who had been badly hurt. She attended to him and seeing he was in a serious condition went to get assistance. On returning, it was evident that he was too ill to be removed, and in a few minutes he died on the spot where she had found him.

All her hopes of future happiness were now shattered and she finally decided to give up army life and return home. She obtained a pass to England and eventually landed in Dublin.

Nothing is known of the fate of her children or of how she became so impoverished that she had to open a small beer and pie-house in Dublin. She received a pension of a shilling a day, which was afterwards reduced by the Lord Treasurer to fivepence. Later on she returned to London and first kept a pie-shop in Westminster and afterwards a public-house in Paddington. Her adventurous career as a soldier made her famous and brought many customers, including certain noble patrons who asked her to their houses—more for a joke than anything else—so that she could entertain the guests with her stories.

In the end she took asylum in Chelsea Hospital, where she lived out her last years in peace. She died there after reaching the great age of one hundred and eight years. She was interred according to her wish among the old pensioners with military honours, and three volleys were fired over her grave.

So ended the life and career of this remarkable woman whose determination and courage make her conspicuous among the others of her sex ; a woman who played the part of a man and who fought with great bravery in the British Army.

VIII

THE bloodthirsty life of a pirate on the high seas was hardly likely to attract even the most adventurous woman, yet according to records left by Captain Charles Johnson there were at least two who followed that calling, dressed in sailors' clothes, and who lived and fought in desperate frays in the early eighteenth century.

The first of whom we have an account is Mary Read, who is said to have been born in England. Her mother who was married to a sailor when she was quite young ; when he went on a voyage not long after the wedding was left with a baby boy to keep. As she was very poor, she thought of going to London with the object of finding her husband's mother, whom she had been told was in good circumstances and therefore might perhaps provide for the child. But before she could carry out this plan the boy died. Later on, she gave birth to a girl whom she named Mary, and being still desirous of getting help from her mother-in-law, who was expecting her with her boy, she had to decide what was the best thing to do.

The changing of a girl into a boy to deceive an old woman was difficult but not impossible, she thought, and so after dressing Mary in boy's clothes she brought her to London and presented her to her grandmother as her husband's son. The grandmother was pleased with the child and would have taken it, but Mary's mother, pleading that it would break her heart to be parted from her, came to an agreement whereby the child was to live with her and the grandmother was to allow a crown a week for her maintenance.

70

The change once made, it was difficult to go back, so Mary's mother decided to continue to clothe her and bring her up as a boy. When the grandmother died Mary's mother was again reduced to poverty, and she was obliged to put the girl into service, which ended in her being placed with a French lady for whom she worked as a foot-boy. She was now thirteen and had grown up sturdy and strong. Being both bold and courageous she had a great longing to rove the world and leave domestic service, so when she was old enough she left her situation and entered herself as a hand on board a man-of-war on which she served for a time as a sailor. Later, she left the ship, crossed to Flanders and enlisted in a regiment-of-foot as a cadet. The cadets at that time were volunteers who generally served without pay, hoping to obtain a commission if they proved suitable.

Although Mary behaved with courage and bravery she was unsuccessful in gaining a commission, but she managed to obtain an exchange to a regiment-of-horse. Here she served with distinction and behaved so well in several engagements that she earned the commendation of her officers.

She fell in love with one of her comrades, a Fleming, a dashing young fellow who had no idea of her real sex. She began to spend much of her time with him, neglecting her duty of keeping her weapons clean, and was constantly getting into trouble. When her troop was ordered out on foray she used to accompany it without permission if her sweetheart was there, and in this way she ran into frequent danger. The other soldiers, not suspecting the reason, began to think she had gone crazy, but it was not long before Mary made the young man aware of her sex, for they shared the same tent and were constantly together.

At first he was greatly surprised and not too pleased ; then he became importunate, but Mary knew how to take care of herself and resisted all his temptations. This only served to increase his ardour and at length he besought her to marry him. As this was Mary's desire she agreed, and when the campaign was over and the regiment marched into winter quarters she exchanged her uniform for the clothes of a woman and they had a public wedding.

The story of the two troopers who had married each other became the talk of the camp and caused such a stir that they resolved to leave the service. As there was nothing against them and they had gained the favour of the officers, they were soon able to get their discharge.

With the little money they had received in gifts and with what they had saved, they opened an eating-house called ' The Three Horseshoes ' near the Castle of Breda. They soon established a good trade with the officers of the regiments quartered near, but their prosperity did not last very long, for Mary's husband died, and when the Peace of Ryswick was concluded the military left Breda and she was forced to give up the business.

As her money was nearly all gone Mary decided to resume man's attire, so she dressed herself in one of her husband's suits and journeyed to Holland and enlisted in a regiment-of-foot quartered in one of the frontier towns. After a time, seeing no chance of promotion, her roving spirit again asserted itself, and she resolved to go abroad and seek her fortune.

She got her discharge from the regiment and, making the coast, she shipped on board a vessel bound for the West Indies. For a time all went well on the voyage, but one day a ship bore down on them, hoisted her flag, the dreaded skull and cross-bones, and demanded the vessel's surrender. They could offer little resistance, and under the command of the notorious Captain Rackham the pirates boarded the vessel

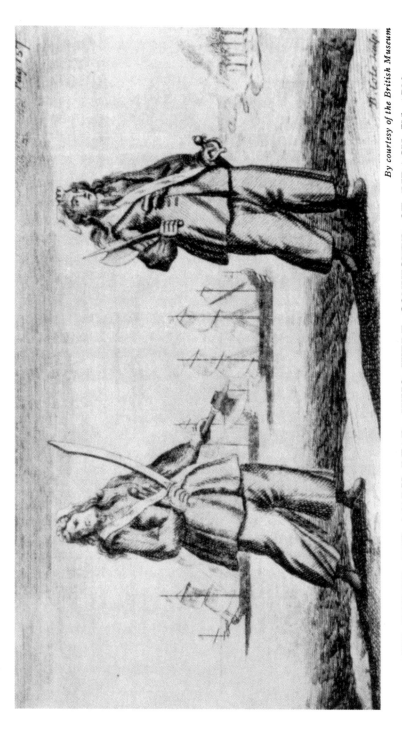

ANN BONNY AND MARY READ, WHO WERE CONVICTED OF PIRACY IN 1720

(From an engraving by B. Cole.)

MARY ANNE TALBOT
(From a lithograph dated 1809.)

and after plundering her, let her go. Mary, the only English person among them, they kept, and took her on board the pirate ship. Having no alternative, she threw in her lot with the pirates and worked as a sailor until she was landed at New Providence in the Bahamas, where she remained for a while.

At length she took advantage of the King's Proclamation, published in all parts of the West Indies, for pardoning all pirates who would voluntarily surrender by a certain day ; with the rest of the crew she gave herself up to the authorities and for a time lived quietly on shore. But Mary could not remain idle for long. When she was getting short of money again she heard that Captain Woodes Rogers, the governor of the Island of Providence, was fitting out some privateers to cruise against the Spaniards, and she with several others determined to join and resume their roving life. They embarked, and on reaching the island had little difficulty in joining a ship forming part of the expedition.

Captain Rackham was in command of their vessel, and they had no sooner sailed than the crew mutinied and reverted to their former occupation of piracy. Mary Read remained with them, although she always declared that the life of a pirate was repugnant to her and that she was always on the look-out for an opportunity to leave it. Her sex was apparently never suspected by anyone on board, but among the crew there happened to be another woman in man's clothes, whose name was Anne Bonny. She took a great liking to Mary, whom she admired as ' a handsome young fellow.' Mary on becoming aware of this sensed her danger and at length confided the secret of her sex to Anne.

The intimacy which had sprung up between the two supposed young men disturbed Captain Rackham, who was Anne Bonny's lover, and he grew intensely jealous and threatened to cut Mary's throat until Anne, afraid he might carry out his threat, let him, too, into the secret. Rackham was satisfied, and he carefully kept the secret from the ship's company, and the friendship between the two women continued.

During the cruise the pirates took a great number of ships belonging to Jamaica and other parts of the West Indies, bound to and from England. Whenever they found a good craftsman on board, if he was not willing to join them they compelled him.

On one of the vessels they took prisoner ' a young fellow of so engaging appearance ' that Mary took an immediate fancy to him which developed into a violent passion. She could not rest night or day, and, as she found her affection was reciprocated, they became mess-mates and such close companions that at length Mary revealed the secret of her sex to him. Her love grew no less strong than his, but one day the young man quarrelled with one of the pirate crew while the ship was at anchor near the islands. They resolved to fight it out there and then on shore. Although Mary was anxious as to the fate of her lover, she would not let him refuse to fight as he might have been branded with cowardice, so she resolved to pick a quarrel with his opponent herself. Having challenged him ashore, she fixed the time of their meeting two hours in advance of the time arranged for his fight with her lover. The duel began with pistol and cutlass, and Mary with her first shot killed her opponent on the spot.

When the ship at length put into port, Mary married the man of her choice in a church and together they went to sea again in Rackham's ship, and were engaged in many fights. The intrepid Mary knew no fear and was usually in the forefront during the attacks at sea when the vessels were at close quarters. In one battle, when most of the crew were drunk down below, Mary and Anne Bonny, with one man, kept the deck alone, calling out to those below to come up and fight like men. When she found they did not appear, she fired her pistols down the hold killing one and wounding others. The pirate ship was at length captured and the crew were made prisoners and taken to Jamaica.

Of the adventurous life and career of Anne Bonny, the woman-pirate who so often fought by the side of Mary Read, but little is known.

Anne Bonny was an Irish girl who was born in Co. Cork, where her father practised as an attorney-at-law and her mother was a lady's maid. Owing to domestic trouble Bonny realized all he had and embarked from Ireland with his child Anne and Caroline, a maid, to seek his fortune in America.

On landing, he began first to practise his profession again, and then went into trade. Fortune so favoured him that he was soon able to buy a large plantation. The maid Caroline, who passed as his wife, died shortly afterwards, and his daughter Anne kept house for him.

She grew up to be a fine, strong girl and proved her courage and determination on several occasions, but she had a fiery temper which often got her into trouble. It was rumoured that she had killed a maidservant with a clasp-knife in one of her passions, and that she had beaten a young man who waylaid her until he was prostrate ; but when not provoked, she was said to be a good and dutiful daughter.

Although her father was ambitious that she should make a suitable marriage, for she would inherit his wealth and estates, she disappointed him by falling in love with a good-looking young sailor who arrived one day in Charlestown. Knowing she would never gain her father's consent, she married him secretly ; when her father learned of this, he was so enraged that he turned her out of the house, and declared he would have nothing further to do with her. The bridegroom, who had not a penny, realizing his wife would never get her father's money, slipped away to sea without even bidding her good-bye.

After Anne had recovered from her surprise on his disappearance a new aspirant for her hand came along in the person of Captain John Rackham, the handsome, daredevil pirate who was known as ' Calico Jack.'

Anne was carried away by his impetuosity and she agreed to go to sea with him, but in order to do this she was obliged to dress in men's clothes so as to keep her sex concealed from the rest of the crew.

They sailed off on a piratical honeymoon, which continued for some time, when from certain news conveyed to the Captain by Anne he made for Cuba, where he put her on shore in a small cove where he had a house and some friends. After the baby was born, he went to Providence to take advantage of the Proclamation pardoning pirates who surrendered, but before long he again took command of a privateer, and Anne returned to the ship, again dressed as a sailor.

She was as active as any of the crew when an engagement took place and fought courageously with cutlass or marlinspike. She joined in their carouses and when a prize was taken was the one to serve round rum to the jubilant victors.

In October 1720, while sailing near Jamaica, the pirates were surprised by the sudden arrival of an armed sloop which had been sent out by the Governor of the island with the object of capturing Rackham and his ship.

A fight followed, and while most of the crew, except Anne and Mary Read, were down below decks they fought gallantly, as already related.

The pirate-ship was captured and the two women, with Rackham and the rest of the crew, were taken as prisoners to Jamaica. They were tried for piracy at

St. Jago de la Vega and convicted on 28 November 1720. They were all sentenced to death.

On the day Rackham was executed, by special favour Anne was allowed to see him. She told him she was sorry to see him there, but ' if he had fought like a man he need not have been hanged like a dog.'

Although Mary Read was convicted and sentenced like the others she was not executed, as she died in prison of fever before the sentence could be carried out. Anne Bonny pleaded to have her execution postponed on account of her condition and this was granted, after which nothing further is known beyond the story that she, too, was seized with a violent fever and ended her days in prison.

ALTHOUGH there are several instances on record where a woman posing as a man has played the part of husband to another of her sex, one of the most amazing cases of this kind was that of Mary East, who, under the name of ' James How,' lived as a married man with a woman for nearly thirty-five years.

Mary East was born about 1715, and when she was seventeen fell in love with a young man for whom she had the strongest affection. Although he wished to marry her, he had no means to support a wife, and in his despair resolved to take to the road and turn highwayman. His career in that capacity, however, was soon cut short, for before long he was arrested for highway robbery. He was tried, found guilty, and condemned to death. The sentence was commuted to transportation for life, and after 1732 Mary never saw him again. She was so stricken with grief and disappointment that her hopes of a married life had been dashed to the ground, that she made a firm resolve to remain single for the rest of her life.

Close to where she lived there happened to be another girl who had met with several disappointments in love and who had formed a similar resolution. By a curious coincidence the girls became known to each other. They were soon firm friends, and as their intimacy grew, they exchanged confidences. Since they were both of one mind they made a pact to live together, and they carefully thought out the most prudent method of procedure.

Eventually they decided that one of them should

dress in men's clothes and that they should go and live as man and wife in a neighbourhood in which they were not known.

The first difficulty that arose was which of the two should play the man. They agreed to decide the matter by drawing lots, and it fell to Mary East to assume the masculine role.

They were both about the same age and were strong and well-built, but of the two, Mary appears to have been the sturdier and better adapted to assume the male character.

They managed to scrape together about thirty pounds, and with this capital resolved to set out on their travels on foot.

Mary equipped herself with male clothes, cut her hair short, and with a pipe complete had a fair resemblance to a young man of twenty who was to be known in future as ' James How.' When they reached the neighbourhood of Epping they chanced to see a small inn to let which they decided to take and, after getting possession, they remained there for some time and ran the business.

Little is known of their life at this time, beyond that ' James How ' got involved in a quarrel with a man in the district and on entering an action against him, obtained a verdict in his favour and got five hundred pounds damages. With this addition to their capital, they resolved to stay in the business and find a better place to carry it on. They fixed on a prosperous public-house in Limehouse Hole which they bought ; they moved in after having disposed of the inn at Epping. Each took a part in the management of the business and they were regarded by their customers as a model couple, and so gained the respect of all in the district.

At length, by hard work and saving, the pair managed to put by a considerable sum of money. As their business increased they added to their capital, and invested it in another public-house called the ' White Horse ' at Poplar. This also proved a success and they acquired several subsidiary inns which they supplied from the ' White Horse.'

There they lived together in harmony for about eighteen years, until one day a woman who had known Mary East in her youth, saw and recognized her. She found out where she was living and discovered that she was not married to her supposed husband, whose antecedents she also traced. She resolved to turn this knowledge to account by blackmailing Mary, and began by writing a letter to ' Mr. James How ' asking for fourteen pounds to be sent to her or she would make a public disclosure of all she knew concerning the pair. In terror at this demand, Mary sent her the money and for some time she remained free from further threats. Meanwhile ' James How ' continued to gain the respect of his neighbours and served in most of the parish offices in Poplar, with the exception of that of churchwarden and constable, from which he was excused on account of an injury to his hand. In spite of his effeminate appearance no suspicion as to his true sex appears to have been aroused and he served several times on juries and was elected as foreman.

About Christmas 1764, the woman who had previously blackmailed Mary made a further attempt and demanded another ten pounds to keep her secret, and the couple sent it in the hope of stopping the disclosure which they believed would ruin them. Emboldened by her success, the blackmailer repeated her demand a fortnight later, and ' James How,' not having sufficient money in the house and fearing the threat, sent her five pounds. Worried by this trouble, the female partner was taken ill and went to the house of her brother in Essex in the hope of recovering her health, but she got worse and sent for ' James ' to

come to her. Before he could arrive, she told her
brother the truth, that ' James ' was not her husband
but a woman dressed as a man. Her death followed
shortly after.

The blackmailer, fearing now that Mary would not
yield to her demands, formed a new plan to make her
pay, and for this purpose hired two ruffians to assist
her in carrying it out.

One of these, a mulatto, passed as a court officer, and
the other, equipped with an official staff, was supposed
to be a constable. In these characters they presented
themselves at the ' White Horse ' and asked for ' Mr.
How.' Mary came forward in her usual male attire,
and they told her that they had been sent by Mr.
Justice Fielding to apprehend her for a robbery committed about thirty years previously, and that they
were also aware of the secret of her sex.

Mary, conscious of her innocence of any charge of
robbery, was terrified at the threat to disclose her
secret, and while she was wondering what to do
she saw an intimate acquaintance passing the
door, and she called out to him. He was a Mr.
Williams, a pawnbroker, whom she had known and
respected for some years. Drawing him into an inner
room she quickly informed him of the business of the
two men who were still waiting outside. She swore
to him that she was completely innocent of any charge
of robbery, and at the same time told him how she had
posed as a man for many years. When he had
recovered from the surprise caused by her confession,
Mr. Williams declared she should not be arrested on a
false charge and that she should not be taken before
Sir John Fielding until she had appeared before their
own bench of magistrates. Promising to return in a
few minutes, he left her and went to his shop to make
arrangements to accompany her. When the two men
saw him go, they came in and renewed their threats,

but at the same time, told Mary if she would give them
£100 they would give her no further trouble ; if not,
she would certainly be hanged for the crime within a
week. They were to receive £40 each for bringing her
to justice.

She remained firm in resisting their demands, waiting anxiously for Mr. Williams to return. Several
minutes passed and, as she still refused to give
them any money, they seized her by force, rushed her
out of the house and carried her through the fields
towards Garlick Hill, where the woman who had employed them lived. There they compelled her under
further threats to give them a draft at short-date on
Mr. Williams for £100, after which they let her go.

Meanwhile her friend had returned to the ' White
Horse,' to find her absent, and had set off immediately
to the police court, to see if she was there ; failing
to find her, he had at once hurried on to the court over
which Sir John Fielding presided, with like result.
Returning to the ' White Horse,' he found that Mary
had come back almost in a state of collapse, with her
arms bruised and clothes torn.

She told him all that had happened and promised to
act on his advice. He allayed her fears and said he
would wait and see the course of events.

On Monday, 14 July 1763, the woman blackmailer
in whose favour Mary had drawn the draft called on
Mr. Williams to ask if he would pay it, as it became
due on the following Wednesday. He told her that
if she would call and bring it when it was due he would
see about it. Meanwhile he applied to the magistrates
for advice, and on the Wednesday in question, a
constable was sent to his shop with orders to be in
readiness. The woman duly arrived accompanied by
the mulatto. They were both at once arrested and
taken before the magistrates then sitting at the
' Angel,' in Whitechapel. There Mr. Williams,

accompanied by Mary, now dressed in women's clothes, were waiting.

The woman and her confederate were soon brought before the bench, and in the course of her examination, she stoutly denied that she had sent for £100 ; but the mulatto swore she had sent him for that amount—otherwise why would he have gone on such an errand ? Proof of the attempt at extortion and assault were given by Mary and the prisoners were committed to Clerkenwell Sessions.

The relatives of Mary's partner now laid claim to her share of the property, for she had told them before she died that they had made between three and four thousand pounds, part of which was invested in the business and part in stocks. Mary duly acknowledged their claim and paid them over half of her capital. It was afterwards stated by those who had known the couple, that during the thirty-four years they had lived together in this remarkable partnership, neither one or the other of them had ever been observed to dress a joint of meat, nor would they allow any meetings to be held in their houses. They never kept any servants and Mary East (as the man) always used to draw the beer, serve, fetch and carry all the pots, and do the rough work.

Mary, now dressed in the attire of her sex, decided to retire and, after selling her businesses and settling her affairs, she went to live in another part of Poplar to enjoy the results of her labour and live on the property she had acquired in her strange partnership. She lived to the age of sixty-four years, and died in January 1781. She left most of her money to a friend who lived in the country and some to a young woman who had served her as maid after her retirement. She also bequeathed fifty pounds to the poor of Poplar, fifty pounds to a working gardener she knew, and her gold watch to a Mr. Curry, a distiller in the same district.

THE extraordinary lure of the sea and a spirit of adventure led girls as well as boys at one time to brave the dangers of a sailor's life. Some of the women, however, who became both soldiers and sailors, were led by force of circumstances to conceal their sex and adopt the life of a man.

A strange case of this kind was that of Mary Anne Talbot, a woman shown by her remarkable career to have been both brave and valiant, and with a determination that would have been a credit to a member of the sex she assumed.

She is said to have been the natural daughter of Earl Talbot and the youngest of sixteen children, her mother having died in giving birth to twins. She was born in London on 2 February 1778, at a house in Lincoln's Inn Fields, and for the first five years of her life she was placed in the charge of a nurse, in a village about twelve miles from Shrewsbury. When she was older she was sent to a boarding-school kept by a Mrs. Tapley in Foregate Street, Chester, where she received her early education where she remained a pupil for nine years.

Her only surviving sister, who was married to a Mr. Wilson of Trevalyn, in Derbyshire, lived not a great distance away, and Mary regarded her as her parent until one day when she was about ten years old, Mrs. Wilson told her the truth and showed her a miniature of her mother. The face made a lasting impression on the child's memory, and she never forgot it. Her sister also told her that before her mother's marriage she was known as the Honourable Miss Dyer, the name of the family in which she had been brought up, and she had possessed a fortune of £30,000 besides a yearly income of £1500.

Mrs. Wilson died soon afterwards, and within three months of her death, a Mr. Sucker of Newport, Shropshire, became her guardian, and removed Mary from school and placed her with his own family. Here her life was most unhappy and she was treated with great harshness. Sucker was an arrogant and domineering man and the girl had an absolute dread of him. It was soon evident to Mary that he wished to get rid of her and his responsibility. Later, he introduced her to a Captain Essex Bowen of the 82nd regiment-of-foot and directed her to consider him as her future guardian. The Captain declared he would arrange for her further education as he was greatly interested in her family and would take her abroad.

Early in 1792, he took her to London and arranged to stay at the Salopian Coffee-house near Charing Cross. Captain Bowen introduced Mary to the landlady as his ward, but before many days had elapsed he took advantage of her innocence and seduced her. After this his benign attitude changed and he began to treat the girl with unkindness and even cruelty. Mary had neither acquaintance nor friend to appeal to in London, and, left to the mercy of a tyrant, she was obliged to carry out his harsh commands.

Suddenly, an order came for him to rejoin his regiment, which was to embark for St. Domingo, and Mary began to hope her troubles were over, but Bowen informed her that he intended to take her with him. It was impossible for him to take a girl with him on the ship, so he insisted that she should dress as a foot-boy, or servant, so that she might accompany him on the voyage to the West Indies. He called her ' John Taylor,' and under that name she sailed in the transport as his servant in the ship *Captain Bishop* on 20 March 1792.

Once on board the Captain had to alter his attitude towards the girl, but he treated her with his former harshness and compelled her to live and share the mess of the ship's company.

The voyage proved a terrible one and the *Captain Bishop* encountered severe gales in the Atlantic. She sprang a leak and all hands had to be called to the pumps, while guns and provisions had to be thrown overboard. For eight days they were without water and reduced to a ration of a biscuit a day each person, but the weather moderated and at last they reached land in safety.

In spite of all the hardships and privations which Mary faced with indomitable courage, she managed to keep her secret and dressed as a boy was successful in concealing her sex.

The regiment had scarcely landed at St. Domingo when new orders were received to re-embark and return to Europe, to reinforce the troops under the Duke of York in Flanders.

Under a threat of sending her up the country to be sold as a slave, Bowen compelled Mary to enrol herself in the regiment as a drummer. There was no escape, and in that capacity she sailed again with Bowen for Europe. He continued to use her as his servant when her duties as drummer permitted.

Eventually the ship arrived at Flanders and the regiment was at once marched to a camp, where frequent engagements were taking place and the soldiers were undergoing considerable suffering. From day to day, Mary was exposed to fire, and towards the end of the siege of Valenciennes she was hit by a musket-ball between the breast and collar-bone, and was also wounded in the small of her back by a blow from the sword of an Austrian trooper.

Terrified that her sex would be discovered if she went to hospital, she carefully concealed her wounds and treated them herself with basilicon ointment, lint, and some Dutch drops she managed to obtain. Fortunately for her, Captain Bowen, who had treated her so shamefully, was killed in the attack on the town. She set out to search for him and found him among the dead on the battlefield. On examining his pockets she found several letters referring to herself, and, in his wallet, the key of a case in which he kept his papers. In this case she discovered part of a correspondence that had passed between Bowen and Sucker, and evidence that money which had been sent for her use had never been handed over to her. These documents she carefully preserved by sewing them up under the shoulders of her shirt.

She had no friends in the regiment, and sick and unhappy she determined to desert and try and reach England. She managed to obtain some sailor's clothes, and as soon as an opportunity occurred she abandoned her drummer-boy's uniform, and, dressed as a sailor, set off by night across the country. The tramp was long and arduous, but at length she reached Luxembourg.

She found the city was in the possession of the French, and as she could obtain no work, through sheer necessity she shipped on a French lugger that was just sailing. She sailed in September 1793, and it was not long before she found out that the vessel was a privateer. She underwent great hardships on the ship, which cruised about for four months until in the Channel it fell in with the British Fleet commanded by Lord Howe.

When the ships engaged, the intrepid Mary went to the French captain and told him she would not fight against her countrymen, to which he replied with a sound beating with a rope's end, but to her relief the lugger soon surrendered and a boarding party carried off the captain and crew, including Mary, to the *Queen Charlotte*, the Admiral's ship. Here Mary was fortunate enough to be able to relate her story to the Admiral himself. She told him of her service in the Army, and how owing to privation she had been forced to ship on the French lugger, but had determined to escape at the first opportunity in order to return to England.

Lord Howe, impressed by her candour and courage, believed her story and promised her she should have her desire, for he would transfer her to another ship. Mary was delighted, and especially since she had been able to keep the secret of her sex concealed.

She was soon after sent on board H.M.S. *Brunswick*, commanded by Captain Harvey, where she was instructed to act as powder-boy on the quarter-deck. Her quickness and obedience, together with her smart appearance, at length attracted the attention of the Captain. He thought she was a lad who had run away to sea, but finding she was well-educated and had seen active service on land, he made her his principal cabin-boy.

He took a strong liking to his sharp and nimble new boy, who became a favourite with the ship's company. Mary was in many fights, and, in the action in which Captain Harvey later lost his life, she took an active part. Just before his ship was engaged by the *Ramillies* she received a severe wound in the leg by a grape-shot. She fell and lay wounded on the deck and while almost unconscious received a musket-ball in the thigh. Suffering acute pain and weak from loss of blood she was at length carried to the cockpit. The busy surgeon made but a cursory examination and decided to send her to port as soon as possible with others severely wounded.

The *Brunswick* sailed for Portsmouth and when she

reached Spithead Mary was taken to Haslar Hospital, where the bullet was extracted and she remained a patient for four months.

During this time Captain Harvey did not forget her or lose interest in his ' cabin-boy,' for he sent her money and made frequent inquiries as to her progress.

When she was well enough to be discharged from Haslar, she was drafted as a midshipman to H.M.S. *Vesuvius*, commanded by Captain Tomlinson, whose ship was attached to Sir Sydney Smith's squadron. They sailed from Spithead, and when off Dunkirk the *Vesuvius* fell in with two French privateers. Captain Tomlinson, maintained a running fight for seven hours but being outnumbered by the enemy, had at length to give in. Mary, with others, was made prisoner, and, with another midshipman named Richards, she was taken to Dunkirk on one of the privateers and lodged in prison. Here they were treated with great harshness and kept in a damp dungeon. After a while they made a plan to escape which unfortunately miscarried and they were discovered. As punishment they were confined for eighteen months in separate cells where it was so dark they did not see daylight for eleven weeks. Mary's daily ration of bread and water was lowered down by a cord and her bed consisted of a bundle of straw which was never changed. It is little wonder that she became very ill, but while recovering she received better treatment and was allowed to mix with other prisoners. Among those with whom she came in contact was a German who was permitted to occupy his time with making trinkets with gold wire after the style of filagree work. After watching him closely Mary learned the art, which proved to be an aquisition of great use to her later when she gained her liberty and returned to England. Years afterwards, when she settled in London, she got work from a jeweller named

Loyer in Denmark Street. Here she made the bracelet chains which Queen Charlotte wore in the Royal procession to St. Paul's Cathedral, to commemorate the great naval victories.

Some five weeks after recovering from her illness, Mary obtained her liberty through an exchange of prisoners. Her intention was to get a passage in a ship for England as soon as possible, but the spirit of adventure innate in her again asserted itself. Happening to hear a man inquiring for a lad willing to go to America as a ship's steward, Mary volunteered and at once struck a bargain with him. He was a Captain Field, master of the *Ariel*, an American merchantman. He agreed to give Mary fifty pounds besides what she could make as a steward from passengers on the voyage from Dunkirk to New York.

The *Ariel* sailed in August 1796, and during the voyage Mary was treated with great kindness by the Captain. He proved a real friend and when they landed insisted she should come and live with his family at his home on Rhode Island. While there his young daughter fell violently in love with the youthful steward. She even proposed they should get married and tried her utmost to get Mary to consent, but the latter was determined to put an end to this embarrassing position and she fled from the Fields' house. She had not got more than two miles away when she was overtaken by a servant who begged her to return at once as Miss Field had been seized with alarming fits. Mary returned to find the love-sick maiden prostrate, but on giving the girl a promise that she would speedily return from England, she soon recovered.

She then went with Captain Field to New York to rejoin his ship, and after a good voyage the *Ariel* arrived in the Thames in November, 1796.

They soon obtained a fresh cargo and were due to sail for the Mediterranean, when Mary came in for a new adventure. While in port the Captain had engaged a couple of new hands and she, as steward, was deputed to see them and take their descriptions. She saw them in the cabin where money and bank notes were lying about on the desk. In the middle of the same night, Mary was woken by a crash at the upper cabin door. She felt alarmed and snatched at her tinder-box to get a light, when close by she noticed there lay a brace of pistols. A more violent attack was then made on the inner door behind which she was standing, and recollecting that a sword was hanging near her bunk, she seized it just as the door gave way to the attackers. She made a thrust, and although she heard neither groan nor cry, she was sure she had wounded someone. She now struck a light, but the attackers had fled, and after making the door secure she stood on guard till the morning.

Later she learnt that one of the new hands had been found in his berth with a deep wound in his thigh which he said he had got by accident. He was in such a serious condition that he had to be taken to St. Thomas's Hospital. Mary, however, had no doubt how he came by the wound.

A few days before the ship was due to sail, Mary, wearing her sailor's clothes, went on shore with the mate. Just as they landed at St. Catherine's stairs they fell in with a press-gang who seized them both. As Mary obstructed them and fought for her liberty she was thrown out of the boat and received a wound on the head from a cutlass. They were held by the gang and put on board a tender near by. The mate, having his ' protection ' paper in his pocket, was soon liberated, but Mary was less fortunate, for she had left hers on the ship. The mate, however, stood by her, and declared his companion was an Englishman ; but that did not satisfy the officer in charge and in the end she was obliged to reveal her sex in order to get free.

After she returned to the ship and she imparted her secret to the astonished Captain Field. He again treated her with kindness and discretion and told her he wished her to continue on as steward and return with him to America ; but Mary, disheartened, and feeling she could not continue in her role as a man, had to decline his proposal. She left the ship after thanking him for all his kindness to her and bade him good-bye.

Now, alone in London, with no friends, she debated what to do for the best. She first decided to make an application to the Navy Pay Office at Somerset House to see if she could get the money due to her for service while on board the *Brunswick* and the *Vesuvius*. Giving the name of ' John Taylor ' she interviewed the clerks only to meet with repeated rebuffs and rudeness. This at length aroused her temper and she turned and abused them in violent language accompanied by personal chastisement, and as a result she was conveyed to Bow Street. When brought before the magistrate she repeated her complaints of the treatment she had received and was discharged, but several people in court who had heard the story of her sufferings came to her aid. Among them they raised a subscription sufficient to pay her twelve shillings a week until she had got her money from the Navy Pay Office. One of the gentlemen thus interested in her found her lodgings and placed her in charge of the landlord. At the same time he advised her to wear female dress and give up masculine habits. But this did not come easy to Mary, who for so long had worn trousers and assumed the manner and habits of a man, and she continued to go about in her sailor's rig-out.

As her story became known, ' John Taylor ' bid fair to become famous, and now, having a little money, she used to frequent the theatres and coffee-houses in the neighbourhood of Covent Garden, where she was a popular visitor.

One night in a coffee-house she became acquainted with Haines, the notorious highwayman, although she had no idea of his criminal career. When seated at the same table one evening she happened to mention she was at the end of her money.

" Damn it, my fine fellow," exclaimed Haines, clapping a hand on her shoulder, " I'll put you up to the best way in the world to get the cash you stand in need of."

Leaving the house together shortly afterwards, Haines proposed an adventure on the road and gave Mary some money to equip herself for the purpose, as he took exception to her sailor's clothes. She therefore went off and bought herself a pair of buckskin breeches and top-boots, which she at once donned. A rendezvous was fixed and she met Haines and found him accompanied by six other desperadoes. They gave her a brace of pistols and were all ready to start when for once Mary's courage failed her and she resolved to give up the adventure and not embark on a career of crime.

Having but little money left she sought some kind of employment, and remembering the gold wire-work she had learnt at Dunkirk she applied to Mr. Loyer, a jeweller in Denmark Street, who finding she was clever in making filagree engaged her for a time, but paid her very poorly. ' At the time of my employ by Loyer,' she tells us, ' I put on my seaman's dress and accompanied the procession when their Majesties went to St. Paul's, and the different colours of the enemy were carried to be hung up in the Cathedral as trophies of the victories of Howe, St. Vincent, and Duncan. I was one of Lord Howe's attendants with his colours and rode on the car. The chains on the bracelets which Her Majesty wore on the occasion were made by me at Loyer's by order of Grey and Constable, the jewellers of Sackville Street, Piccadilly.'

About this time she joined a lodge of Odd Fellows
that met at the ' Harlequin ' in Drury Lane, although
the fraternity little knew their new member was a
woman.

Mary remained on in the same lodgings until
February 1797, when the leg which had been wounded
with grape-shot began to trouble her again. It became
so bad that she sought and obtained admission to
St. Bartholomew's Hospital, where, after several pieces
of shot had been removed, she was discharged. Later
on, however, the wound began to give her further pain
and she became a patient at the Middlesex Hospital.
While there she heard one day that a woman was
attempting to impersonate her and trying to pass herself off as ' John Taylor who had fought in the
Brunswick.' Suspected of being an impostor she was
arrested and charged at Bow Street. Hearing that
Mary was an inmate of Middlesex Hospital, the
magistrate sent for her to confront her impersonator.
When the woman saw her she confessed to the
imposture and was committed to the house of
correction.

On her discharge from the hospital Mary again
assumed woman's clothes, and one day in the street
she was suddenly attacked by a man who worked as a
hairdresser and who mistook her for someone else.
He knocked her down, cut her head, kicked her, and so
hurt her wounded leg that she had to be taken to
hospital again. The man was arrested and charged at
the Quarter Sessions with committing a brutal assault.
He was sentenced and ordered to pay Mary ten pounds
as compensation. Meanwhile she had a narrow escape
of losing her leg at the hospital, where the surgeons
thought it might be necessary to amputate it. Her
extraordinary career and sufferings now became
known to some influential visitors, who brought her
case to the notice of the Royal Court with the result that

to her delight she was granted a pension by Queen Charlotte, and also received help from the Duke and Duchess of York and the Duke of Norfolk.

When she was once more able to get about, her old spirit revived, and she resolved to try and ascertain what had become of the inheritance which was supposed to be coming to her. With this object she set out for Shrewsbury to see if she could find Mr. Sucker, her supposed guardian, at Newport. Failing to find him, she returned to Shrewsbury, determined to make him see her, and hiring an ensign's uniform and a horse she rode back to Newport. Arriving at Sucker's home she sent in a message that a gentleman knowing the late Captain Bowen wished to see him. She was asked into a room, and shortly Sucker, whom she could hardly recognize, came in. She saw he had no idea who she was and asked him if he knew a ' Miss Talbot ' or could give any information about her. Sucker replied that he had known the lady well, but that she had died in 1793.

Mary, unable to conceal her anger any longer, declared herself to the astonished man and proved her assertion by a mark on her forehead. Sucker stared at the soldierly figure confronting him in amazement, and Mary, determined to frighten the man who had treated her so badly, drew her sword and demanded he should give her an account there and then of the money of which he had defrauded her. Throwing up his arms he declared he was a ruined man and rushed from the room.

Seeing it was useless to pursue him Mary returned to Shrewsbury with the object of consulting a lawyer. Determined to gather more particulars about her family she again paid a visit to Newport, but on arrival at Sucker's house she was informed that he had suddenly left his home and had been found dead at a village nearby.

With very little money left, Mary decided to abandon her quest and return to London. On a suggestion that she should go on the stage, as she had a flair for acting, she became a member of the Thespian Society, which had a theatre in Tottenham Court Road. Here she played ' Juliet ' and ' Floranthe,' and in low comedy took the parts of ' Mrs. Scout ' and ' Jack Hawser.' After one of her performances she was summoned for wearing hair-powder without a licence, which was an offence against the law at the time.

More trouble came to Mary, when she got into arrears with her rent and at the instance of her landlady, to whom she owed eleven pounds, she was arrested and taken to Newgate.

During the time she was in prison she used to preside at the evening convivial meetings held within the walls of the gaol in those days. Dressed as a man she would sing, smoke, and drink with the others, and so became very popular. She was eventually liberated by the ' Society for the relief of persons confined for debt,' on the payment of five pounds.

Ill-fortune, however, still pursued her, for one night in September 1804, she was thrown out of a coach in Church Lane Whitechapel, and falling into a hole in the road she received a broken arm and other serious injuries. She was unable to obtain any compensation and, being without employment, she became a domestic servant in the house of a publisher, where she lived for three years.

Though still a young woman, the hard life which she had led and the sufferings she had undergone now began to tell on her health and she was seized with a great weakness which ended in a complete collapse. She died on 4 February 1808, in her thirtieth year.

Curiously enough this remarkable woman retained much of the sensibility of her true sex during the long period in which she passed as a man, in spite of her association with the roughest type of men on land and sea, and those who knew her always testified to her generous disposition, kindness of heart, and good nature. Her courage was ever undaunted, even when she was exposed to the greatest danger, as she undoubtedly was at the siege of Valenciennes, when she saw hundreds of her friends and foes falling round her. She used to tell how ' the 11th Dragoons fought with their broad-swords hand-to-hand over the heaps of dead and dying soldiers,' and would recall how she was obliged to keep a continual roll on her drum to drown the cries of those who were trampled to death under the feet of the horses.

D URING the last quarter of the eighteenth
century there was a public-house in Wapping,
London, well known as ' The Widow in
Masquerade or the Female Warrior.' A signboard
hung over the door with a picture of a British tar on
one side and a marine on the other. It was kept by the
redoubtable Hannah Snell, a woman whose extraordinary and adventurous life dressed as a man had
earned her the title of the ' Female Warrior.'

Hannah was the daughter of a hosier and dyer and
was born in Fryer Street, Worcester, on 23 April 1723.
Her grandfather had been a soldier and served under
William III and Queen Anne, being fatally wounded
at Malplaquet. As a child Hannah loved to play at
soldiers and used to tell her companions she was going
to be a soldier when she grew up. They generally
appointed her to be chief commander in their games
and called her group ' Amazon Snell's Company.'

After losing both her parents in 1740, Hannah came
to London to live with one of her sisters, Mrs. Gray,
whose husband was a carpenter carrying on his business in Ship Street, Wapping. Here she met and fell
in love with a Dutch sailor named James Summs and
married him at the Fleet on 6 January 1743.

The marriage proved a most unhappy one, for
Summs turned out to be a thorough scoundrel, and not
only spent all his wife possessed, but ran heavily into
debt. Within twelve months, when Hannah was
expecting a baby, her husband deserted her, and to add
to her trouble her child only lived seven months and

she was left alone. She again went to live with her sister, but after a while made up her mind to try and find her husband, of whom she was still fond in spite of the way he had treated her.

To carry out her quest she resolved to dress as a man, and, donning a suit of her brother-in-law's clothes, she set out on 23 November 1745 to walk to Coventry, where she thought she might get news of the missing Summs. On her arrival in the town she made inquiries, but was unable to obtain any information as to his whereabouts. Having come to the end of her money Hannah decided to keep her sex concealed and look for a job.

The town was full of soldiers on a recruiting campaign for General Guise's regiment, and one day she joined a crowd of people around a man with a drummer. While she stood there, a corporal named Bishop asked her if she would ' go for a soldier.' He put a shilling in her hand and invited her to have a drink, and afterwards insisted she should go with him to his captain. Hannah was bewildered for a time, but her old military ardour asserted itself and she marched off with the corporal to see Captain Miller, of Guise's regiment, who was quartered at the ' Bear and Ragged Staff.'

In front of the Captain the corporal swore his new recruit had accepted the ' King's picture ' and was liable to serve, but Hannah spoke up and said she was quite willing to serve her King and country if she was acceptable. Captain Miller then gave her a guinea and five shillings, and the next day she was sworn into the Army before a magistrate.

She enlisted under the name of ' James Gray,' and, after some three weeks drilling, she was marched off with seventeen other recruits for the seat of war, then at Carlisle. The journey north took twenty-two days, which Hannah did without difficulty. At

Carlisle she was again drilled and put under a course of military exercises in which she acquitted herself so well, she was appointed to Captain Miller's company.

Among her comrades there was a man called Davis, who asked her one day to help him in an intrigue he was carrying on with a girl, and although Hannah agreed, she privately informed the intended victim of the plot Davis was hatching against her. Through this Hannah gained the confidence of the girl and their frequent meetings excited the jealousy of Davis, who thought he had been outwitted. In revenge, he seized an opportunity of charging his supposed rival before the commanding officer with neglect of duty, and 'James Gray' was sentenced to receive six hundred lashes. Her hands were tied up to the castle-gate and she had received five hundred when some officers interceded for her and the remainder of the cruel punishment, which was quite unmerited, was remitted.

Not long afterwards a new recruit, a native of Worcester, was drafted into the company, and to her dismay, Hannah recognized him as a carpenter who had lodged at the house of her brother-in-law. Fearing her sex would now certainly be discovered she resolved to take the first opportunity of deserting. Having borrowed some money she slipped away early one morning, and, heading south with Portsmouth as her goal, she set out on her journey.

She knew she was running a great risk of capture on account of the uniform which she was still wearing, but when she got about a mile from Carlisle fortune favoured her, for she saw some men gathering peas in a field, their coats being piled some distance away. She quickly seized the opportunity and exchanged her regimental tunic for one of the old coats and went on her way. She stayed a night at Liverpool and walked on to Chester, where she got a lodging and so ingratiated herself with the landlady that she managed

HANNAH SNELL
(From an engraving by J. Faber, dated 1750.)

'DR. JAMES BARRY'
Inspector-General of army hospitals.   Died 1865.
(From a drawing.)

to obtain some more money ; but in Winchester, where she had an intrigue with a widow, the woman was one too many for her, for she rifled Hannah's pockets one night and left her with but a few shillings. Footsore and weary after walking for a month she at length reached Portsmouth, where she found lodgings for a time with a Mrs. Cunningham, whose husband was a drum-major. She made up her mind to re-enlist so as to be able to get abroad ; she boldly went to the depôt and joined as a marine in Captain Graham's company attached to Colonel Fraser's regiment.

In about three weeks time they were drafted to the East Indies, and Hannah, with the rest of the company, was ordered on board the sloop *Swallow*, which belonged to Admiral Boscawen's fleet. She served as a servant, or boy, to Lieutenant Richard Wyegate, who treated her with kindness and afterwards proved a real friend to her. She soon became popular with her mess-mates on account of her excellent cooking and readiness to do mending for them, and was an equal favourite with the crew of the ship, who regarded her as a boy. In case of an engagement her station was on the quarter-deck to fight at small arms, as she was one of the after-guard. The duties allotted to her included keeping watch for four hours night and day, and frequently she had to go aloft.

During the voyage the *Swallow* encountered a terrible storm and was nearly wrecked. She sprang a leak and all hands were ordered to man the pumps, including Hannah, who insisted in taking her turn with the others and won praise from the officers for her courage and endurance. However, in time, better weather came and the *Swallow* got safely to the Cape of Good Hope, although food ran very low and only a pint of water a day was left for each man.

The Admiral next bore away for Fort St. David on

the coast of Coromandel where the Fleet duly arrived. Hannah, with the rest of the marines, was then disembarked, and after a march lasting three weeks joined the British Army then encamped before Area-Copong. It had been decided by the General to take it by storm, but owing to the bursting of a shell which blew up the magazine, the siege had to be abandoned. Before the camp was struck Hannah was greatly pleased at being again commended for her courage and ready obedience to orders.

The Army then marched to attack Pondicherry, the next objective. The place was besieged for eleven weeks, the men meanwhile suffering great hardships, for rain fell in torrents and they were so surrounded by floods that the attack had to be abandoned for a time. When the weather improved and the attack was renewed, Hannah was the first in the company of English-foot to ford the river, which was breast-high and under constant fire from a French battery. She was then ordered on picket-guard and was on duty continuously for seven nights in succession, and, further, worked hard for fourteen days in digging trenches.

In the next engagement she nearly lost her life, for she formed one of the attacking party, standing knee-deep in the water which flooded the trenches. She had fired thirty-seven rounds during the fight, when she received six shots in her right leg and five in the left. She also received a wound in the groin, and fearing the surgeon might discover her sex on examining her, she got hold of a negress whom she had befriended. To this woman she imparted her secret and persuaded her to procure dressings for the wound. The negress raided the surgeon's medicine chest and got lint and ointment, and between them they managed to extract the balls with finger and thumb. This was acutely painful, but Hannah bore it all, for her secret remained undiscovered, and to her delight the wounds began to heal and later she got quite well again.

Meanwhile, the greater part of the Fleet had sailed, and Hannah was drafted on to the *Tartar Pink* and worked as a sailor until the ships returned from Madras, when she was transferred to H.M.S. *Eltham* and sailed in her to Bombay. Bad weather was encountered, during which the vessel sprang a leak and had to heave-to to repair the damage, which took five weeks.

The Captain remained on shore, and one day during his absence Lieutenant Allen, who was in charge, asked Hannah to sing to the ship's company, but she refused, pleading she was unwell. He tried to persuade her, but as she resolutely declined to concede to his request, she made him an enemy for life. Some time afterwards, having been suspected of stealing a shirt belonging to one of her comrades, he ordered her to be put in irons. After being kept a prisoner for five days she was ordered to receive twelve lashes and was sent to the topmast for four hours.

She took this punishment without complaint, but had the satisfaction of clearing her name when the missing shirt was afterwards found in the chest of the man who had said that she had stolen it from him.

Her mess-mates frequently joked with Hannah on account of her having no beard or whiskers and often called her ' Miss Molly Gray.' This used to alarm her, as she thought some of the men had begun to suspect her true sex, and so that her conduct should not give rise to suspicion, she threw herself into all the fun of the crew and even joined in their drinking orgies. They soon dropped the name of ' Molly Gray ' and dubbed her ' Hearty Jimmy ' instead.

On the voyage to England the ship put into Lisbon, and one day when she was on shore, Hannah met an English sailor who had come from Genoa on a Dutch vessel. In conversation with him she obtained news of her missing husband and learnt that he had been in prison at Genoa on the charge of killing a distinguished man in that city. In the end he was thrust in a sack weighted with heavy stones and thrown into the sea. She now realized she would never see Summs again and was indeed a widow.

At length H.M.S. *Eltham* sailed for home and directly Hannah landed at Spithead she set off for London, where she received a warm welcome from her sister.

She met several of her old mess-mates and after she had received her pay, in an unguarded moment, when she was probably under some more potent influence, she revealed the secret of her sex to one of them. He at once offered to marry her, but she declined and sent him off after he had given her a promise to respect her confidence.

Meanwhile, the story of Hannah's career as a soldier and sailor became known and she was the talk of East London. She had to earn some money for her living, and, as she had a good voice, she decided to put it to account and go on the stage.

She obtained an engagement at the Royalty Theatre in Well Close Square and made her first appearance as ' Bill Bobstay ' in a rollicking sailors' play. She also took the part of ' Firelock,' a soldier, and in that character went through all the military exercises she had been taught in the Army. As ' Bill Bobstay ' she appeared in her uniform as a marine, complete with all accoutrements, and surrounded by her company playing pipe and drum, she marched to and fro across the stage as if on parade. Then she went very smartly through her drill and finished by singing one of her popular ballads, of which the following is an example :

' Hannah in briggs (breeches) behav'd so well
Nor was her Policy confounded
When near the Mark of Nature wounded

Which proves what then will scarce admit
That women are for secrets fit.
That healthful Blood could keep so long
Amidst young fellows hale and strong
Demonstrates, tho' a seeming wonder,
That love to courage truckles under.
O how her bedmate bit his lips
And marked the spreading of her Hips
And curs'd the blindness of his youth
When she confess'd the naked truth !
Her fortitude to no man's second
To woman's Honour must be reckoned.
Twelve wounds ! 'Twas half great Cæsar's number
That made his corpse the ground encumber.
How many men for Heroes nurst
Had left their colours at the first.
'Twas thought Achilles' greatest glory
That Homer rose to sing his Story ;
And Alexander mourn'd his lot,
That no such bard could then be got—
But Hannah's praise no Homer needs
SHE LIVES TO SING HER PROPER DEEDS.'

After another engagement at Sadler's Wells Theatre
Hannah got tired of performing on the stage and gave
it up, after which she again resolved to dress as a man
and wear masculine clothes for the rest of her life. She
bought a smart blue coat which she usually wore with
a laced hat, cockade and ruffles, and always carried
a sword at her side.

In response to a petition setting forth her adventures
and service which was sent to the Duke of Cumberland,
she became an out-pensioner of Chelsea Hospital, and,
on account of the wounds she had received at Pondicherry, was granted a pension of thirty pounds a year.

Her last venture was to take a public-house at
Wapping, for which she had a signboard painted with
a British tar on one side and a brave marine on the
other, while beneath was inscribed : THE WIDOW IN
MASQUERADE OR THE FEMALE WARRIOR.

She attracted many customers, who were all wishful
to see and shake hands with so brave and courageous

a woman. A wealthy lady admirer became god-mother to her son and educated him.

After a time the strenuous life she had led for so many years and the hardships she had undergone on sea and land began to tell on her health. She commenced to show signs of mental trouble and was at length admitted to Bethlem Hospital, Moorfields, where she died on 8 February 1792, at the age of sixty-nine. She was buried in the grounds of Chelsea Hospital, where a portrait of her still hangs in the Great Hall.

THE great popularity and vogue of the masquerade during the eighteenth century probably had something to do with the fashion for wearing strange costumes and impersonating other people, which appears to have been almost a craze among a certain class during part of that period.

The masquerades organized by the notorious Heidegger at the King's Theatre in the Haymarket, received the approval of George I, who had a great liking for this kind of entertainment. Others which drew great crowds were held at Almack's, Boodles, Saunderson's, and at the Thatched House Clubs, while thousands thronged to Vauxhall and Ranelagh when the masked fêtes were held.

The grand masquerades held at Carlisle House, in Soho Square, by Mrs. Cornelys, were also a great source of attraction and were attended by members of the Royal Family, foreign ministers, and the first nobility of the land. It was quite common at some of these functions for women to appear in the costumes of men and for men to assume the attire of the opposite sex.

At length the masquerades became such a scandal that they were forbidden, for, as Steele sagely remarked : ' They had a bad tendency to give a loose turn to a young lady's imagination, for being in disguise takes away the usual checks and restraints of modesty. Ladies might possibly forget their own selves in such strange dresses and do that in a personated character which may stain their real ones.'

The escapades of Annabella Parsons, a famous beauty

and young lady of easy virtue, who became the mistress of the Duke of Grafton, the grandson of Charles II, brought her into notoriety about 1760. Annabella was the daughter of a tailor in a good way of business in Bond Street and from an early age gave signs of becoming a great beauty. When she was about seventeen, her parents sent her in charge of a duenna to Paris to finish her education and so become acquainted with the manners of good society in the French capital.

Here her first adventure proved unfortunate, for in spite of the duenna, she became entangled with a supposed nobleman who turned out to be a rogue and robbed her of three hundred pounds worth of jewellery and valuables.

On returning to London she resolved to seek a more humble environment and became a chambermaid with a family living in St. James's. After she had been there about three months she became acquainted with a Captain Horton, a wealthy West Indian planter, who promised her a handsome settlement if she would give up service. She accepted, and he installed her in luxurious apartments in Green Street, Leicester Fields. Here she lived in grand style, keeping two maids, a cook, and a footman, while in less than three months a carriage and coachman were added to her entourage. She was both artful and clever and easily prevailed on the Captain to take her on a voyage to Jamaica, and they embarked in one of his own ships. They took with them all the fine furniture from their apartments, including the carriage.

After their arrival they took up residence in a large house near one of the Captain's plantations, where Annabella astonished the local society by her fine dresses, beauty and accomplishments.

For a time all went well, but the Captain became very jealous on discovering that Annabella was casting eyes on and growing too friendly with a young planter.

In the end, in exasperation, he called his rival out and wounded him in a duel.

He locked the fair Annabella up in her room as punishment for her infidelity, her only attendant being a faithful Creole woman called Quashi. She made up her mind to escape, and taking the opportunity when the Captain was visiting one of his estates, with the help of Quashi she engaged a passage on a ship bound for Montego Bay. From thence they shipped to Charlestown and eventually got back to England.

Annabella, who had saved some money, at once took lodgings in Pall Mall, where her style and beauty soon made her famous and attracted many admirers, among them being Lord March and Lord Littleton. Later she removed to Hill Street, Mayfair, where she first met the Duke of Grafton, who became deeply enamoured and was a constant visitor to her house. He took her everywhere and introduced her at his private parties, where, we are told, ' her behaviour and ready wit made her a great favourite.' Owing to her close association with the Duke she became known in town as the ' Grafton Beauty,' but Lord March, who had been a former ardent admirer, again sought her out and started another intrigue which lasted until his ardour cooled, when he sent her a hundred-pound note ending their friendship.

After making it up with the Duke she pretended she had a legal right for his maintenance, and on obtaining £500 from him, went off to Paris in January 1768. While there she received a letter from him expressing his great anxiety about her, saying he would dispatch his confidential servant on the King's yacht, which would bring her safely across the Channel.

She arrived in London in time to accompany the Duke to Newmarket, where, after winning several races with his horses, he presented her with another five hundred pounds.

For a short time she settled down, but her flighty character soon led her into another escapade with a young man she met at Ranelagh. When the Duke heard of this he was so enraged he attacked and wounded the youth and carried off Annabella to his house and locked her up in a room.

Among the young women who visited the house was one Diana Davis, whose beauty and accomplishments made her a great favourite with the sporting nobility. She was also an adept in the art of intrigue, and one day brought with her a young Frenchman whom she introduced to Annabella as having come to London to dispose of a collection of valuable laces.

As Diana surmised, he soon fell a victim to Annabella's charms, and together they concocted a little plot to deceive the Duke. The young Frenchman had a very fair and feminine appearance and the women persuaded him to dress in girl's clothes, and when attired like themselves one day introduced him to the Duke as a young French lady from Paris. The Duke was greatly taken with the new arrival and gave her an invitation to stay at his house. No one was aware that the charming French lady was a young man except Annabella and Diana, who were in the secret. As they expected, the amorous Duke took an immediate fancy for the fascinating foreigner, who after leaving his house took lodgings at Kew.

Here 'Mademoiselle' invited Annabella to stay with her for a month and the Duke accepted the same invitation and accompanied them. One morning, however, the Duke surprised the pretended young lady in Annabella's room, and flying into a rage rushed out of the house, ordered his carriage and immediately drove back to town. Annabella was now out of favour, and the Duke, in spite of profound apologies, would not see her and forbade her his house.

For some time Annabella could not think of any

means of reconciliation, until one day she hit on a plan for obtaining admission to his presence. She had figured at several masquerades in male costumes and uniforms ; she now resolved to impersonate a certain 'Captain Sinclair' whom she knew had been a frequent visitor to the Duke's house. Borrowing a suitable uniform and making herself up to resemble the Captain, she boldly presented herself one evening at the house. After being admitted, she was conducted to the library by a footman, who on throwing open the door announced : ' Captain Sinclair.' The Duke was sitting at his writing-table and looked up in frank amazement at the figure which marched in.

Annabella came to a halt before him, clicked her heels, and gave him a smart military salute. " You saucy hussy ! " exclaimed the Duke, as he stared at her, and then, seeing the humorous side of her intrusion, burst into a hearty laugh. Annabella saw she had won. She had a passion for dressing in male attire whenever she could get an opportunity, and as the quarrel with the Duke was now patched up, she often appeared at the masquerades as ' Captain Sinclair.'

Once more in favour with the Duke, all her efforts were now directed in keeping him from other distractions and in preventing his defection, as she imagined that she had prescriptive right to his affections.

Before long, however, to her dismay she found he was paying ardent attention to a Miss V——. Annabella resolved to take steps to prevent this from going any further, and calling some of her theatrical friends together they evolved a plan. Hiring a coach and pair, in which the part of the coachman was played by Mr. Holland, an actor, she attired herself as a clergyman with a wig, shovel hat, and a long, black clerical coat. With a bundle of sermons bulging from the pocket, she was driven in style to the lady's address, where she was announced as a doctor of divinity and was shown into the presence of Miss V——.

The pseudo-clergyman told her he had seen her among his congregation and had fallen in love with her at first sight and wished her to marry him. The young lady was greatly astonished at this declaration, but was favourably impressed by the good-looking clergyman and appeared to be overwhelmed by his offer. She told him it was all so sudden that she would have to consider the matter, but she promised to see him again.

This was enough for Annabella, who next day informed the Duke that she had discovered that his friend, Miss V——, had got another suitor very different from himself. He had made honourable overtures to her which had been favourably received, and she advised him to abandon the pursuit of the fair one and leave it to his more successful clerical rival. This ruse proved successful in cooling the Duke's ardour.

Annabella's extravagance next began to give the Duke some anxiety, and as he wished to marry again, he sought to find her a husband. He told her that if she really loved him as she professed, she would leave him now without making any trouble and he would provide for her. Annabella saw her reign was over and soon without warning she left his house and went to Greenwich to stay with friends. One day, when walking in the park with one of them, a footman came up to her and said his master had sent him to request the favour of her company to take a dish of tea, as he had something important to tell her. Annabella, much intrigued by the message, consented, and leaving her friend followed the footman to a large house on Blackheath. Here she was received by a gentleman with great cordiality and entertained in a richly furnished drawing-room. He told her he was a captain of one of His Majesty's ships of war and he had seen her on several mornings as he rode through the park and been struck by her beauty. He besought her to come and pay him a long visit, but said he would give her time to consider his offer and settle her affairs. To do this he placed his chariot at her disposal for her return to London. Through her friends, Annabella made inquiries about her new admirer and found he had a reputation for great generosity, and lived in grand style with a large staff of servants. She soon made up her mind and in four days she returned to Greenwich and took up her residence with the Captain.

For a few months all went well, then suddenly their alliance was interrupted by an order from the Admiralty for him to proceed with his ship to the Gulf of St. Lawrence. His affairs had to be settled up quickly, and that being done he took an affectionate farewell of Annabella, leaving her as tenant in his house with its valuable furniture and a thousand guineas to support herself, with a promise of an ample settlement on his return.

So Annabella was left to her fate. Owing to her extravagant habits and expenses with the house and servants, she soon ran through the thousand guineas, and within six months after the Captain's departure she found herself forced to sell all the costly furniture, discharge the servants, and leave the house.

Now with little money left she returned to London and took a small house in Pimlico. Her only hope was to bring about a reconciliation with the Duke, and at length she managed to see him. Although he appeared to have a genuine affection for her he proved inexorable on this occasion, and earnestly entreated her to leave the country as soon as possible and not to lay him under the necessity of ' taking measures to hasten her journey.'

Annabella, in tears, saw he was determined and that the end had come. She submitted to his proposals and left him for the last time to make preparations for her journey. The Duke treated her very generously and provided for her immediate needs ; after she had settled abroad he sent her large sums of money from time to time. Later it is stated she returned to England again and eventually became Lady Maynard.

IT is curious how the Army appears to have been a source of attraction to many of the women who posed as men a century or more ago. The risk of detection was great, yet several enlisted as soldiers and saw active service, showing by their courage and bravery they could endure the hardships of a campaign as well as any man.

While few ever attained high rank there was one woman (whose real name is still a mystery) who rose to become a full Inspector-General of the Army Hospitals.

Posing as a man and assuming the name of ' James Barry ' she passed the whole of her career without her true sex being discovered, until death revealed her secret. She is said to have been the granddaughter of a Scottish Earl and to have been born in 1795, but no authentic account of her parentage is known.

Some light is thrown on Barry's early days by Dr. Jobson, who was a fellow-student with ' him ' at Edinburgh. He states that ' James ' persistently avoided his fellow-students and used to be laughed at because, instead of the shooting-coats which all the other students wore, he dressed in a long frock coat. He lived in Edinburgh, with his mother to whom Dr. Jobson was introduced. Both he and Barry resolved to go into the Army and were together at a depôt. Jobson was an athlete and was disappointed that he could not get Barry to box. ' He ' would never strike out, but kept his arms over his chest to protect it from blows. ' When Barry died, it was discovered she was a woman and had been a mother,' says Dr.

Jobson, ' I was as astonished as anyone, for I never had the slightest suspicion as to her real sex. What romance or tragedy led to this impersonation has never transpired.'

Down to the end of the eighteenth century there was no efficient system of ambulance for British troops and it was customary, if a soldier was badly wounded on the field, for the officer commanding his company to order one or two of his comrades to carry him to the rear for medical attention. If the regiment was actively engaged, wounded men remained uncared for on the ground until the fighting ceased. There was no specially trained corps for ministering to the wants of the sick and wounded, but a few soldiers from the ranks were sent when necessary to act as attendants on the sick, and these were called hospital orderlies. Even during the Peninsular War in Wellington's time our wounded were usually carried from the field on stretchers by bandsmen of the regiment, and afterwards transported to the hospitals in the rear in carts of the commissariat, or in hired bullock-wagons. In 1854, at the time of the Crimean War, there was little or no improvement in attention provided for the wounded, but in 1855 a medical-staff corps was formed. Previously all ambulance duties, as well as nursing in the military hospitals, had been carried out by the hospital orderlies.

Such was the condition of things when young ' James Barry ' joined their ranks. He is said to have shown a remarkable aptitude for the work. He was quick in grasping the facts and had a facility for acquiring knowledge, and these qualities were the dominant features of his character.

His rise was rapid, for in 1819 he was made staff-surgeon and on 22 November 1827 was raised to the rank of Surgeon-Major.

He saw considerable foreign service during his

career and was sent to the Cape of Good Hope in 1819 to act as medical adviser and staff-surgeon to the Governor. It is at this time that we get the first description of this remarkable person, which is given by the Earl of Albemarle in his book entitled *Fifty Years of My Life*.

He writes : ' At this time (1819) there was at the Cape a person whose eccentricities attracted universal attention. He was Dr. James Barry, staff-surgeon to the Garrison and the Governor's medical adviser. Lord Charles described him to me as the most skilful of physicians and the most wayward of men. He had lately been in professional attendance on the Governor, who was somewhat fanciful about his health, but the Aesculapius, taking umbrage at something said or done, had left his patient to prescribe for himself.

' I had heard so much of this capricious gentleman that I had a great curiosity to see him. I shortly after- wards sat next to him at dinner at one of the regimental messes. In this learned Pundit I beheld a beardless lad, apparently of my own age, with an unmistakably Scotch type of countenance—reddish hair and high cheek-bones. There was a certain effeminacy in his manner which he seemed to be always striving to overcome. His style of conversation was greatly superior to that usually heard at a mess-table in these days of competitive examination.

' A mystery attached to Barry's whole professional career, which extended over half a century. While at the Cape he fought a duel and was considered to be of a most quarrelsome disposition. He was frequently guilty of flagrant breaches of discipline, and on more than one occasion was sent home under arrest, but somehow his offences were always condoned at head- quarters.

' The late Mrs. Ward, daughter of Colonel Tidy, told me that she believed the doctor to have been the legitimate granddaughter of a Scotch Earl, whose name I do not now give as I am unable to substantiate the correctness of my friend's surmise, and that the *soi-distant* " James Barry " adopted the medical profession from her attachment to an Army surgeon who has not been many years dead.'

Barry also served at St. Helena, the Ionian islands, Malta, and in the West Indies, and although eccentric in some ways he is said to have displayed on various occasions great skill in dealing with the sick. He had the reputation of being ' very touchy ' and quarrelsome, which often brought him into conflict with his brother-officers, and it was one of these quarrels that led to the duel he fought when at the Cape.

One who knew Barry very well by sight, says : ' She lived some forty years in Down Street, Piccadilly, and it was a matter of common repute that " he " belonged to the other sex. She was about five feet six inches in height and had a smooth, pale face. She was a great friend of Lady Charles Somerset, who lived close by in Piccadilly.'

An Army officer who served on a Court Martial with Barry in 1844 thus relates his impressions at the time : ' I was sent from the Barbados to Trinidad, to sit on a general Court Martial, and on the assembly of the Court an individual appeared who at once attracted my attention. He was in the full-dress of an Army surgeon, but had all the appearance of a woman.

' On making inquiries I was told he was Dr. Barry, principal medical officer of the district.

' The impression and general belief was that he was a hermaphrodite. I was under the belief there had never existed a true hermaphrodite, so I was convinced Barry was a woman of about sixty years of age. Being interested I cultivated his acquaintance and we became very friendly. I endeavoured to draw out his antecedents, but he was very reticent. The only thing

I discovered was that Lord Fitzroy Somerset (afterwards Lord Raglan) was a friend of his, and I inferred that it was through him that Barry had obtained his high position.'

General Chamberlayne, who knew Barry in Jamaica, says in his *Recollections* : ' I do not think she wore a ring. Her hair was light—I think dyed—but very thin and cut close. She wore high-heeled boots. She had a queer fondness for animals, keeping several dogs and cats very happily. She was rather bombastic in speech and repellent in manner, but kind and anxious to do good to those who were not likely to become intrusive.

' When I think of the anxiety, care, and trouble she must have experienced for years to keep up the assumed character, possibly first undertaken for the love of some man and then subsequently retained perhaps for the sake of his character, it seems surprising that she possessed so many good points.'

Colonel Wilson, who remembered her, says : ' I recollect that, like most women, she loved attending weddings and christenings. When I was Foot-adjutant in Jamaica, I frequently met her at dinner at General Ashmore's and we were all much amused at the outrageous stories she used to tell, making herself out quite a lady-killer. At balls or parties she was certain to tack herself on to the finest and best-looking woman in the room. She dyed her hair red, but had none on her face.'

Concerning ' Dr. James Barry ' a writer in *The Lancet* states : ' I travelled with this remarkable character on board the inter-colonial steamer plying between the islands of St. Thomas and the Barbadoes, when I occupied the same cabin. I in the top and he in the lower part. I well remember how in a harsh and peevish voice he ordered me out of the cabin while he was dressing in the morning.

' " Now then, youngster, clear out of my cabin while I dress," he would say.

' A goat was on board to provide him with milk, for he was a strict vegetarian. He was accompanied by a negro servant and a little dog called Psyche. The doctor was at the time travelling to visit an old friend and enemy, General Sir Josiah Cleote, commanding troops, with whom, when aide-de-camp to the Governor of the Cape, he had fought a duel and was wounded in the leg.

' The late Colonel Shadwell Clerke, who was at that period on the General's staff, told me before his death last year, that he too was challenged by Barry for some fancied insult, but that General Cleote pooh-poohed the idea and made them shake hands.

' Barry was short in stature and angular in figure, with a long Ciceronian nose, prominent cheek-bones, and rather lugubrious expression of countenance.

' He or she always seemed to have immense influence at Headquarters and could almost choose his own station. Imperious in manner and officially dictatorial in social circles, he was admired and respected. He was sympathetic and skilful in his profession—yet what a life of repressed emotions it must have been for a woman who, it was said, gave birth to a child in her early days ! '

In 1857 another person who knew Barry tells us that in appearance and manners he was effeminate. His face and hands were smooth and white like those of a woman and he had no beard or whiskers. He was very irritable, but was able to talk well on most professional subjects. His habits, too, were peculiar. He was a vegetarian in diet and at dinner ate only fruit and vegetables, which he first soaked thoroughly in water, in order, as he said, to remove animalculæ from them.

' He was thin in build and in stature resembled a

'DR. JAMES BARRY' WITH HIS BLACK SERVANT AND
DOG
(From a drawing reproduced in the *Lancet*.)

LADY HESTER STANHOPE
(From a lithograph by R. J. Hammerton.)

JÔON, ON MOUNT LEBANON
The castle where Lady Hester Stanhope lived and died.

woman, with small limbs in good proportion. His voice was shrill and squeaky and was quite unlike the voice of a man. The impression left after speaking with him was that he laboured under some sexual malformation. He is said to have always worn a peculiar and tight-fitting dress, and though he was always attended by a black man as valet, he was very secret with him and would never allow him to be present when he was dressing.'

In 1851, on 16 May, Barry was promoted to be Deputy Inspector-General, and on 7 December, 1858, he was made full Inspector-General of Hospitals. He was placed on half-pay on 19 July 1859 and came to live in London.

In Hart's Annual Army List for 1865, the name of James Barry, M.D., stands at the head of the list of Inspectors-General of Hospitals.

In 1865, he was taken ill and died at Down Street, Piccadilly, London, on 15 July of that year, and the death of Dr. Barry was duly announced in *The Times* of the following day. After his death, Dr. W. A. White, Dr. J. G. David, and Dr. Mackinnon were deputed by the War Office to hold an inquiry into the case, and they reported that the body of ' James Barry ' was that of a woman in every respect. Neither the landlady of the house where she lodged nor the black servant who had lived with her for many years, had the slightest suspicion of her sex.

She is said to have been seventy-one years of age when she died. She was buried at Kensal Green Cemetery.

The sandstone tombstone over the grave is inscribed:

DR. JAMES BARRY
INSPECTOR-GENERAL
OF ARMY HOSPITALS
DIED 15 JULY 1865
AGED 71 YEARS.

It is indeed difficult to comprehend, whatever may have been the reason for the impersonation, how in assuming the attributes of an Army medical officer, she could have so successfully maintained the deception through a long life without detection.

A MONG the remarkable women whose masculine instincts altered the course of her life and eventually led her to live and die in exile, was Lady Hester Lucy Stanhope. She was the eldest daughter of Charles, Viscount Mahon, afterwards third Earl Stanhope, by his first wife, and was born in 1776.

Even in childhood she showed great force of character, domineering over her sisters and generally making herself unpleasant at home—so much so that in 1800 she left her father's house and went to live with her grandmother. She developed into a tall, beautiful woman, and William Pitt, her uncle, attracted by her bold and courageous character, invited her to come and keep house for him. She became his most trusted confidant, arranged his official banquets and receptions, and generally played an important part in the political and social activities of the period.

In 1806, when William Pitt died, he desired that an income of £1500 a year should be settled on her, and soon afterwards she left London and went to live in Wales.

' She would never have her likeness painted when at the height of her beauty,' wrote one who knew her well. ' Her head was a perfect oval ; her brows arched and fine ; her eyes blue approaching grey ; her nose somewhat large and the distance from her mouth to her chin rather too long. Her cheeks had a remarkably fine contour as they rounded off towards the neck, so that Mr. Brummell once said to her at a party : " For God's sake do take off those ear-rings and let us see what is beneath them." She was tall, not far from six feet, rather largely proportioned and was once very plump. Her mien was majestic, her address eminently graceful and her conversation enchanting. She was an excellent mimic and had more wit and repartee than falls to the lot of most women. She had a profound knowledge of human nature and was courageous morally and physically and as proud as Lucifer. She never read more than a few pages of any book, and history she considered a farce.'

Such was Lady Hester in the early years of the nineteenth century. When she was about thirty a change came over her and she developed a still more masterful and masculine character both in manner and appearance. She would not tolerate any interference or social restrictions of any kind, and she determined to go where she would have an entirely free hand in living untrammelled by civilization. To this end, in 1810, she set out for the East accompanied by a young English girl named Williams as companion, a medical man called Charles Lewis Meryon, and several servants.

The party sailed for the Levant on board the frigate *Jason* and was shipwrecked off Rhodes, but in the end they managed to reach Palestine and eventually they arrived at Jerusalem. She did not stay long in the Holy City, but when supplied with equipment she travelled into the desert and around the ruins of Palmyra set up a camp. From thence she moved her site to the slopes of Mount Lebanon, which was at that time peopled by half-savage tribes. Here, after making friends with the sheiks of various tribes, she finally settled down.

She prevailed on the Pasha of Acre to cede her a ruined convent and the village of Dahar-Jôon, situated on a conical mount and peopled by the Druses. Around the convent she built a group of houses surrounded by gardens, and beyond them a strong outer wall of defence so that the place appeared like a fortress.

The Arabs believed she had incredible wealth and from her mountain fastness she ruled the district. She wielded a despotic power over slaves and later even roused the Druses to revolt against the Turks. She knew no fear and posing as a man adopted the dress of the Arabs as well as their customs. Her open-handed charity to all who came to her for relief caused the tribesmen to hold her in the highest veneration.

When her companion died in 1828 all her servants were natives, whom she ruled literally with a rod of iron. This took the form of a mace she habitually carried, and her blows, when she thought them neces-sary, were punctuated with lurid language.

She had a great love for horses as well as for other animals, and kept a large number of cats within the convent walls.

In his *Memoirs of Lady Hester*, Dr. Meryon, who accompanied her on her wanderings and eventually settled down in her abode on Mount Lebanon, throws an interesting light on the life they led at Jôon.

' Long habit,' he says, ' had reconciled me to her eccentricities and even her violent and overbearing temper. The reason she used to give for leaving England was on account of the narrowness of her income, for she declared she could not live on the £1500 a year which Mr. Pitt had assigned to her.'

" When I was young," she used to say, " I was never what you call handsome, but brilliant. My teeth were brilliant and my complexion brilliant."

Although she made a companion of the doctor for years she did not like the profession. She used to say : " I have known many apothecaries cleverer than doctors. There was Chilvers and Hewson, and there was an apothecary at Bath Mr. Pitt thought more of than his physician. A doctor's business is to examine *grandes affaires*, talk to the nurse and see his blister is well dressed, not to talk politics, say such and such a woman is handsome and chatter about what does not concern him."

To show what a distinguished and really Turkish appearance she had, she used to relate that once, while riding her beautiful Arab mare Asfoor near a place called Gezýri, dressed in a crimson burnous with a richly embroidered dress under it, and sitting astride her crimson velvet saddle, she happened to approach an encampment of the Pasha's troops. 'Several " street ladies " who were living with the soldiers ran across a field and came up to me, thinking I was a young bey or bimbashi. Every time, just as they got near I quickened my horse's pace so they might not see I was a woman. At last two of them came and fairly seized my knees so as to make me turn and look at them. But what was their confusion when they saw I had no beard or moustache and was one of their own sex.'

Lady Hester had many distinguished visitors in spite of her isolated mountain fastness, and among them were Lamartine and Kinglake who was struck by her extraordinary appearance. She loved to talk and would do so for hours together, and she liked her hearers to stand while her slaves filled the pipes, or knelt round her in postures of oriental humility while she fanned herself as an Eastern potentate.

Dr. Meryon says : ' I have known her lie for two hours at a time with a pipe in her mouth (from which sparks fell and burned the counterpane with innumerable holes) when she was in a lecturing humour. She would go on in one unbroken discourse like a parson in a pulpit. She harangued one unfortunate English visitor so long that he fainted away from fatigue.'

She could not bear to be alone, and the doctor was her constant companion although she always refused to have anything to do with his wife. She occupied much of her time by physicking her dependants or cutting out garments for all those with whom she came in contact.

Dr. Meryon went back to England for a time, but after his return to Jôon in about twelve months, he found her conducting her establishment in the regular Turkish manner.

On one occasion Lady Hester sent him to see Prince Pückler Muskau, who had written to her asking if he might see her. She sent a message saying he could come when she felt better, but meanwhile she wished particularly to know about a certain serpent's cave.

" You must tell him," said Lady Hester, " that at ten or twelve hours distance from Tarsus there is a grotto where there once lived an enormous serpent with a human head such as may be seen in paintings of Eve. This serpent possessed all the skill in demon-ology and magic known on earth. There was an ancient sage who was desirous of acquiring this serpent's wisdom, which he knew could be come at by destroying the serpent. He therefore induced the King of the country in which the grotto is situated to enter into his views, and by the King's order the neighbouring peasantry assembled for that purpose. The sage had given instructions that in killing the serpent they were to proceed in a particular manner, and that the head was to be preserved for him. He stationed himself close by, and when the peasants went as usual to carry the serpent's food, intending to seize a propitious moment for effecting the destruction of so formidable a reptile, the serpent being gifted with speech said : ' I know what you have come for. You have come to take my life. I am aware I am fated to die now and I shall not oppose it, but on killing me, beware how you follow the instructions of the wicked man who sent you. Do exactly the reverse.'

" The peasant obeyed the serpent and did precisely

the reverse of what the sage had told them to do. The King died, too, ánd since that time no other serpent has appeared with a human head, although several were living in the same grotto and they are still fed by the villagers.

" Now, you must tell the prince that this story is perfectly authentic and that since the time of Sultan Môorad to the present day, certain villages are exempt from taxes in consideration of their providing food for the serpents."

Dr. Meryon told Lady Hester he did not believe the story and declared it was but a crazy tale. Lady Hester replied : " Well, Doctor, look here. You will talk to the Prince a great deal about serpents, and when no one is likely to hear, say in a low voice : ' Lady Hester recommends you to make some inquiries about the serpent's cave when you are at Beyrout, for it is near to where Tarsus Ibrahim Pasha's army is encamped, and this will be a good excuse, as everybody will fancy you had no political motive for going there.' "

She smiled, for the mystery of the fabulous story she had invented was out and Meryon understood it was but her way of revealing one of the deep-laid plots which she had discovered in the neighbourhood and so to save the Prince from being considered as a spy in the dangerous district where the two armies lay.

' Never was there so restless a spirit,' wrote the Doctor. ' Never lived a human being so utterly indifferent to the inconveniences to which she sub-jected others. I was the only English person with her and she made me the vehicle of all her wishes, griefs, and abuses. I controlled her accounts and was her treasurer. I had to discuss medicine with her and was expected to cure an incurable disease as well as to scold her servants.

' One of her servants, called Old Pierre, rendered himself unpopular among the Christians, and at the same time abused the Moslems. The Turks swore they would be revenged and fell upon him with sticks one night. Lady Hester heard his cries for help and commanded the assailants to be brought before her in her *salon,* where she was seated on a sofa with her heavy mace in her hand.

' " I have settled them," she cried later. " My arm has some strength in it yet. I have given them pretty well." '

She then demonstrated to the Doctor with what force she had so effectively wielded her mace.

One day, he tells us, she asked him to go out and talk to a person who was waiting at the gate. He only saw a poor man standing there.

" Ah ! That's the one," cried Lady Hester, " but that's not a man but a woman in man's clothes. She comes here every year for a little money, for at the siege of Acre she used to carry water to the artillery-men on the ramparts so they might drink during the firing. Give her fifty piastres ! "

The thirty cats and kittens she kept were allowed to eat anything and neither fish, flesh, nor fowl could be kept on a shelf but half a dozen cats would be at it, gnawing or carrying it off. When she assumed the costume of a Turk in order to make it quite complete and correct she had her head shaved so that she could wear the red fez and turban.

When war broke out, owing to an insurrection of the Druses against the Turkish Pasha in charge of the district, she sent Dr. Meryon to England with the following characteristic letter addressed to Sir Francis Burdett.

JÔON.

July 20*th,* 1838.

MY DEAR BURDETT,

I am no fool. Neither are you, but you might pass for one if in good earnest you do not understand my letter. A lion in the desert being caught in the huntsman's net called in vain to the beasts of the field to assist him and received from them about as shuffling an answer as I have received from you. A little field-mouse gnawed the knot and called to the lion to make a great effort which burst the noose and out came the lion stronger than ever.

I am now about building up every avenue to my premises and there shall wait with patience, immuned within the walls, till it please God to send me a little mouse, and whoever presumes to force my retirement by scaling my walls or anything of the like will be received by me as Lord Camelford would have received them.

Hester Lucy Stanhope.

By 30th of July the masons had been sent for, and stones and materials had been collected for walling up the gateway. Lady Hester had drawn up a plan showing the exact way in which she required it to be done. It took the form of a screen which completely masked the gateway and left a side opening just large enough for a cow or an animal to enter. The work of immolation was completed, but events proved that she was not to be molested by her turbulent neighbours.

Her lavish generosity caused her to get heavily into debt, and at last she had recourse to Levantine money-lenders who advanced her money on note of hand. After importuning the British Foreign Secretary and receiving no satisfactory reply she appealed to Queen Victoria in August 1838. The last letter she wrote to Dr. Meryon was on 6 May 1839. She then shut herself up in her castle-fortress with some five retainers, walled up the gate and refused to see any visitors. So, alone, without any friend near her, she became deeply depressed, took little food and gradually wasted away.

When almost at the last, news of her was brought to Beyrout and Mr. Niven Moore, the British Consul, together with Dr. William McClure Thomson, an American missionary, set out to ride across the mountains to render assistance ; but they arrived too late. She died on 23 June 1839 before they got to Jôon and they found the fortress deserted, for the native servants had fled, taking with them all the plunder they could carry. Nothing was left in the room where her emaciated body lay but some ornaments on her person which were probably left owing to a superstitious dread of robbing the dead.

The two men tenderly carried her body and laid it in a grave they had dug in the garden, as they thought would have been her wish.

Dr. W. M. Thomson, the American missionary who performed the last rites when Lady Hester was buried, says of her : ' She possessed extraordinary power of conversation and was perfectly fascinating to all with whom she chose to make herself agreeable. She was, however, whimsical, imperious, tyrannical, and at times revengeful to a high degree.

' Bold as a lion, she wore the dress of an Emir, weapons, pipe, and all, nor did she fail to rule her Albanian guards and her servants with absolute authority. She kept spies in the principal cities and at the residences of pashas and Emirs.

' And yet, what a death ! Without European attendant, male or female, alone on top of a bleak mountain her lamp of life grew dimmer and yet more dim until it went out in hopeless, rayless night.'

Thus ended the life of a remarkable woman who, in spite of her eccentricities, had many sterling qualities. Once the gay and brilliant niece of Pitt, presiding in the *salons* of the master-spirit of Europe, and familiar with the intrigues of kings and cabinets, she spurned the conventional rules of the society in

which she had been bred, and violated propriety in
the realization of a singularity in which she gloried.
She had indeed a contempt for her own sex, which
in turn gave rein to her masculine instincts and
characteristics.

XV

WHO was the individual known as ' James
Allen ' who married and lived for twenty-
one years without being detected or arousing
suspicion of her real sex ?   Her identity was never
established and still remains a mystery.

The story of her extraordinary life was revealed
at an inquiry into the cause of her death at St.
Thomas's Hospital in 1829.   In January of that year
a middle-aged couple named Mr. and Mrs. James
Allen were living in Dockhead in the East End of
London.   James Allen worked as a sawyer in Mill
Street close by, and was known as a steady and hard-
working man, and his wife who kept house for him
was a quiet and respectable woman.

The couple had been married for twenty-one years
and had first met when they were both in service
with the family of Mr. Ward, of Camberwell Terrace,
James being a groom and Mary a housemaid.   He was
a smart, good-looking young man and an excellent and
satisfactory worker, while Mary was a favourite with
the family which she had served well for three years.

During the latter part of this period James became
very attentive to the housemaid, and at length he
asked her to marry him.   At first she would not consent
to his proposal, but later on she yielded to his entreaties
and agreed to his wish.

After the marriage had taken place they went to the
Bull Inn in Gray's Inn Lane to stay the night.   Very
soon after they had retired to their room the bridegroom was taken ill and continued to be unwell

133

throughout the night. When he recovered, as they had but little money, Mary found a situation with a Mrs. Lonsdale at Maze Hill, Blackheath. She stayed with her for some time, during which she seldom saw her husband, although they carried on an affectionate correspondence in which he declared he ' was her most loving and affectionate husband until death.' After eight months had elapsed and they had both saved some money, James prevailed on his wife to give up her situation so that they could live together as man and wife. Mary consented, and with their combined capital they bought the Sun Inn at Baldock and went there to live.

The venture proved successful, and as they became popular with the customers the business rapidly increased. For a time all went well, and then one night a calamity happened, for the house was broken into and they were robbed of all the valuables and cash they possessed.

After this misfortune they sold the business at the inn and returning to London took lodgings in the neighbourhood of Dockhead, where James thought he could find work as he had had experience as a ship-wright. He first found employment in a ship-builder's yard as a pitch-boiler, and gained respect as a sober, steady, and active man. Although he had rather a peculiar voice the secret of his sex was never even suspected by his fellow-workers, who had no doubt that he was a man. On leaving this job he went to work in a vitriol factory for a time, and later entered the service of Mr. Crisp, a sawyer, for whom he was working when the accident occurred which caused his death.

More light was thrown on the life and character of this strange person at the inquest held by Mr. Thomas Shelton, the Coroner, at St. Thomas's Hospital on 14 January 1829, to inquire into the cause of his death.

THE FEMALE-HUSBAND

Right : Mary Allen, who lived and worked as 'James Allen' for twenty-one
years.

Left : Abigail Mary Allen, her pretended wife.
(From a contemporary print.)

By permission of the 'Morning Leader'

CATHERINE COOMBES, WHO LIVED FOR FORTY YEARS
AS 'CHARLEY WILSON'

It transpired that the individual who styled himself ' James Allen ' was about forty-two years of age, and had met with a serious accident at his work and died while being taken to the hospital. At the inquest, William Shrieve, a sawyer in the employ of a ship-wright and builder at Dockhead, said he had known Allen for the past two years. On Monday afternoon he saw him at work in a saw-pit in Mill Street. He was on top and Allen below.

They sawed off a large piece of timber, one part of which fell into the pit and struck Allen on the head. He was placed on a shutter and carried to the hospital, but died on the way. He had constantly worked with Allen, and noticed he had a very weak voice and no beard or whiskers. He understood he was a married man and had been so for twenty-one years. Within the last six or eight months he had heard doubts expressed as to the sex of James Allen by people who knew him, and some considered him a hermaphro-dite. He was industrious and hard-working, but did not live on happy terms with his wife on account of his jealous disposition, and for that reason they had parted several times.

Jane Daley, another witness, said she had known James Allen and the female who passed as his wife for a number of years. She never doubted Allen's sex until about eight months ago, when his wife said to her ' she was sure that her Jimmy was not a proper man.'

She knew that he treated the woman badly at times, and she had advised Mary Allen to leave him. She was sure the two were married, for she had seen the certificate, and the ceremony took place at Camberwell Church. She could swear Mary was a real woman and she was as innocent as an infant and did not know she had been imposed upon.

Evidence was then given by Mr. John Martin of

St. Thomas's, who said the deceased was brought to the hospital in male apparel and was quite dead, the cause being a fracture of the skull. On examination the body was found to be that of a female and perfect in every respect. The jury returned with a verdict of ' Accidental death.'

Mary Allen afterwards produced a certificate proving that her marriage to the person called ' James Allen ' had taken place at Camberwell Church on 13 December 1808. She declared that although she had never questioned his sex, she had always suspected that he was an imperfect person, and that whenever she attempted to approach him he always shrank away. Whenever she mentioned to him certain peculiarities he became very angry, so afterwards she never alluded to the matter, but kept her suspicions to herself.

Latterly he was rather bad-tempered and expressed strong resentment if she was noticed by a man and began to act the part of a jealous husband. He even ill-treated her at times, but she considered that since she was married to him and he worked for their living she must put up with his peculiarities.

She had never told her relations of her suspicions. James was very strong and generally dressed in sailor's clothes like a ship-wright. He always wore thick, long waistcoats which extended from the neck to the hips. He had always kept his neck covered, and used to wear a bandage across his chest, for the purpose, he said, of protecting him from cold. He had an ingenious mind, could turn his hand to anything, and was an excellent carpenter. She had never heard him speak of any relatives, but one time he told her he had been born at Yarmouth.

After the inquest, permission was given by Mary Allen for a post-mortem examination to be made on the body, with the result that it was found to be that of a female in every respect. The only feature of a masculine character were her hands, which were very large and hard owing to the kind of work on which she had so long been engaged.

At the funeral of the mysterious ' James Allen ' an immense crowd of people assembled, and a rumour was circulated in the neighbourhood that the ' resurrection men ' were lurking about in the hope of procuring the body of so remarkable a subject for the anatomists. It was decided, therefore, to deposit it in a vault in a private burial-ground in the parish of St. John's, Bermondsey, so as to make access to it impossible. There it was well-guarded and secured against attacks of the body-snatchers.

Mary Allen, who was forty-one at the time of her ' husband's ' death, was left almost destitute, although his comrades at the mill did what they could to help her. During his lifetime he used to receive a little money quarterly, but from what sources she would never disclose. Mary is described as a woman of high character, and had never given James Allen any reason for jealousy, but it was said that nothing roused him to greater indignation than that his partner should ever transgress the rules of decorum when in the company of the male sex, surely a strange complex in a woman who had so long posed as a man.

For some reason a strong feeling of antagonism was aroused among the public against the unfortunate Mary after the death of her ' husband,' and rumours were spread that she had assumed the dress of a woman for the purpose of concealing her sex. This caused one of her friends to appeal to the Press in the following letter which appeared in *The Times* on 19 January 1829.

" SIR,
       I am desired by Mrs. Allen, the surviving associate of that extraordinary female who has for

more than twenty-one years passed as her husband, to contradict the statement made by the club which so far has denied its assistance to her.

I regret, sir, to add that apart from the financial worries of this unfortunate woman (who has been left entirely destitute), she is at this time under great terror through the menaces of a set of unfeeling beings in the neighbourhood, who have expressed their determination to ill-treat her whenever she goes out, as they did on the occasion of the funeral.

Such are the strange vagaries of human nature, that her neighbours should show animosity to an unfortunate woman who finds herself through no fault of her own the supposed widow of another woman who had so deeply wronged her.

'James Allen' was no hermaphrodite, but a woman like herself who successfully concealed her sex until her death."

XVI

AMERICA was not without women who masqueraded as men and served in the armies taking part in the conflict between North and South in the civil war of 1860.

Among them was Loreta Janeta Velazquez, said to have been descended from an old Castilian family of that name, who has left a record of her experiences during the campaign. According to her story she was born in Havana in 1840, and was secretly married in 1856 to a young American army officer. On the secession of the State to which he belonged his wife persuaded him to throw in his lot with the Confederates.

When the war broke out, in the spring of 1860, Madame Velazquez became deeply interested in it, and excited by the struggle about to take place, was determined to have a share in it. Without waiting for her husband's consent she joined his regiment under the name of ' Harry T. Buford ' and became a member of the Independent Scouts C.S.A.

In the account she has left of her adventures she tells us in some detail how she effected her disguise so that her true sex might not be detected. She first donned a coat heavily padded in the back and under the arms to the hips, but when she got to New Orleans she went to an old French army tailor who made for her half a dozen fine wire-net shields. These she wore next to her skin, and over them an undershirt of silk or lisle thread which fitted close and was held in place by straps across the chest and shoulders like braces.

These undershirts were made to be rolled up into the small compass of a collar-box. Around the waist of each of them was a band with eyelet-holes arranged for the purpose of making the waist-bands of the pantaloons stand out. ' With such underwear I used,' she says, ' any woman who can disguise her features can readily pass as a man.'

She observes : ' There were several points about my disguise which were strictly of my own invention, and I do not care to give them to the public. One of the principal causes of my eventual detection, after having successfully passed myself off as a man to thousands of keen-eyed observers, was that my apparatus got out of order and I was forced to dispense with it.'

After she had become accustomed to wearing male attire and appearing before others, she states, she lost all fear of being found out, and learned to act, talk, and almost think as a man.

' Many a time when in camp,' she declares, ' I have gone to sleep with fifty to sixty officers, lying close together wrapped in their blankets, without fear of ·detection.'

Once accepted and complete in her uniform, Lieutenant Buford was instructed to proceed to Hurlburt Station to raise a regiment of recruits. When this was accomplished she entrained for New Orleans, and at Pensacola was met by her amazed husband whom she advised by telegram of her arrival.

Seeing the futility of further argument on her course of action he took command of her recruits and began to train them. Then came a fatal disaster, for one day when he was explaining the use of the carbine to one of the sergeants the weapon exploded and killed him.

Loreta Velazquez was now left alone in the world ; she resolved to carry out her intention of remaining in the Army in the guise of a man. She was determined to see service in the war if her sex remained undiscovered, and was full of enthusiasm for the cause of the Southerners. She succeeded in joining the troops, and took part in the battle of Bull Run.

' The supreme moment of my life had arrived,' she says. ' Fear was a word I did not know the meaning of, and in the engagement the Confederate troops first gave the enemy a taste of their genuine quality and achieved their first great victory.

' I attached myself to my favourite officer, Bee, and remained with his command the entire day. Our men suffered terribly, and at length Bee was compelled to give the order for us to fall back. I was overcome with rage and indignation, but I soon saw the object Bee had in view when he called up his men in the rear of a house and in a voice of thunder cried, " My boys, at them again ! Victory or Death ! See how Jackson stands there like a stone wall ! "

' The expression pleased the men mightily, for they took it up immediately and with a cheer for " Stonewall Jackson " they made another dash for the enemy. The fiercer the conflict grew the more my courage rose, till Bee, at the head of his regiment, fell mortally wounded.

' The conflict became more bitter, but the arrival of the force led by Kirby Smith decided the fate of the battle. The Federals fled defeated, and our army fell back on Manassas Junction.

' After the battle I appealed to General Jackson for the promotion I considered I had fully earned, and he gave me a recommendation to General Bragg for a recruiting commission, but this I did not care about. Finding there was no immediate prospect of a fight I returned to Richmond.'

Soon growing restless with inaction, Loreta next resolved to do some spying, and decided to try and get through the enemy's lines, trusting to her woman's wit to evade capture.

' I have no hesitation in saying,' she writes, ' that I wish I had been created a man instead of a woman, but being a woman I was bent on making the best of it, and having for some time now figured in the garments of the other sex, I resolved for a time to resume those of a female.'

Seeking an old negro woman who had worked for her Loreta told her she intended visiting the Yankees, and asked her to find her some women's clothes. She brought her a calico dress, a woollen shawl, a sun-bonnet, and a pair of shoes, and hid away her uniform until her return ; then, making her way to the river, she got a negro who had a boat to take her across to the Maryland shore, for which she gave him twenty-five dollars.

' It was midnight when we embarked,' she continues, ' and we reached the other side at about four in the morning. I rested under a wheat stack and slept till daylight. Adjusting my clothes I started off, and at length I met a man to whom I said that I had been driven out of Virginia and was trying to get to Tennessee.

' He gave me permission to go into his house, for I was both cold and hungry. His wife gave me some breakfast, and after bidding them good-bye I started for Washington, hoping to pick up some useful bits of information there.'

On her arrival Loreta went to Brown's Hotel, where she was fortunate in meeting an officer of the Federal regular army who had been a personal friend of her husband. He had not the slightest idea why she was in Washington and spoke without reserve. By judicious questioning she succeeded in obtaining some information from him with regard to the operations of the Federal forces in the west, but most important of all was the vital news that active preparations were being made to secure the possession of the upper Mississippi. She also heard that a large fleet was being fitted out to blockade the mouth of the river.

' I succeeded in getting ample confirmation of all my friend told me. I pumped him in a quiet way, and when I left Washington I was fully convinced that a grand blow was shortly to be struck either at Mobile or New Orleans. I did not care to be suspected as a spy, and having fulfilled my errand I left Washington and got back safely to Leesburg, where I sought the old negro woman and got back my uniform in return for the women's clothes she had lent me.'

The next day Loreta was *en route* for Columbus, Tennessee, and eventually she reached Fort Donelson where General Pillow was in command and active preparations were being made to meet the opposing forces.

She says : ' I saw there was much to be done in completing the entrenchments and I determined to lend a hand. My boy Bob and I therefore went into the trenches and commenced to shovel dirt with all possible energy, but I soon found it was work much better done by a man, and with aching back and blistered hands I marched on to the new quarters of General Floyd.

Loreta then describes the great battle which opened on Thursday, 13 February 1862. She says : ' The weather was intensely cold and at night a tremendous storm of snow and sleet came on. The battle raged on. The agonized cries of the wounded and piteous calls for water affected me more than my own discomfort. Every now and then a shriek would be uttered that would strike terror to my soul and make my blood run cold. I could face the cannon better than the bitter weather and the cries and groans of the wounded. My clothes were perfectly stiff with ice and I ached in every limb, but by a resolute effort I stood my ground until relief came and I was able to seek shelter.'

The battle lasted four days, and although the Confederates fought with desperate valour they were at length compelled to yield. The next day the forces on the land side and the gunboats tried what they could do in taking the fort, but without success, and at the end of the second day's battle the Confederates still had the advantage.

After a lull in the storm the Federal forces rallied and rushed towards the entrenchments, and after a severe struggle the Confederates were driven back, leaving hundreds of dead and wounded lying on the frozen ground. Although they fought gallantly the Federals were masters of the field and the Confederates retreated, anxious to save as many of their men as possible from being taken prisoners.

It is said to have been the most terrible battle of the war. In many of the trenches Loreta saw the bodies heaped together six or seven feet high. 'It was sickening to think of the many poor fellows who, after fighting bravely and falling helpless from their wounds, had their lives crushed out by the furiously driven artillery.'

A short time afterwards, during a skirmish with the enemy, Loreta was wounded in the foot and was compelled to have it dressed by a surgeon. She was greatly alarmed in case her sex should be discovered, and she decided to slip away and get to New Orleans.

She had not been there long when she was convinced she was being watched, and this impression turned out to be correct, for she was arrested as a spy and taken before the Provost-Marshal. Her secret was, she feared, on the point of discovery, but she resolved to put on a bold front, reserving a revelation of her identity as a last resort. She was questioned closely by the officer, and then to her relief was released from custody. But her freedom was not for long, for on the following evening she was again arrested on suspicion of being a woman and was taken before the Mayor, a man called Monroe.

She says : ' He questioned me very imperiously in a pompous manner. He simply chose to assume that I was a woman and ordered me to change my apparel. I resolved not to give in without a contest, and turning to him, said, " Sir, prove that I am a woman. It will be quite time when you do that for you to give me an order to change my dress."

' This rather disconcerted the Mayor, and, after a brief consultation, they decided to remand me to the calaboose until it should be settled to his satisfaction what I was, and whether I was a man or a woman. Here I was visited by Dr. Root of the Charity Hospital, and I was soon convinced that his mind was made up and my only method was to confess frankly to the Mayor that I really was *a woman*. I therefore wrote him a note asking for a private interview, which he granted, and I then told him my reasons for assuming the garb I wore. He said he would be compelled to fine me ten dollars and sentence me to ten days' imprisonment.'

Loreta, however, was undaunted even by this set-back, for as soon as possible after her release she went to the recruiting office and enlisted in Captain B. Moses' company of the 21st Louisiana Regiment, and next day was sent off to Fort Pillow to join the regiment. She obtained a transfer to the army of East Tennessee and, receiving her papers, set out for headquarters.

While on her way she and her party came under fire from a detachment of the Federals, who were apparently firing shells at random. A shrapnel burst in the midst of her party, killing one man and wounding Loreta severely in the arm and shoulder. She was thrown to the ground and stunned. When she was picked up by one of the soldiers she found she was unable to use her right arm and was in great pain from the wound. An ambulance was procured and she was put on a train bound for the south. When the train stopped at Corinth she alighted and got word sent to a young surgeon she knew, asking him to come and try to do something to relieve her suffering.

He came directly and examined her arm and she, seeing he suspected her sex and feeling further concealment was useless, told him to his great amazement who she really was. He found that her shoulder was dislocated and that she had other wounds, and after dressing them and putting her arm in a sling he saw her off to Granada.

After her arrival at Indianapolis Loreta occupied her time in working again as a spy in the prison camp, and, disguised as a cake-woman, she later got into the arsenal.

Afterwards she went to St. Louis, and, making friends with a chambermaid, she managed to get into a hotel and ransack the bedrooms where many officers were staying, to search for despatches or orders.

In the end she went to Hannibal, where for a time she gave up her adventurous life, but before the war ended this indomitable woman had a further experience as a blockade-runner.

When hostilities ceased she returned to her home, but did not settle down until she had travelled over Europe and visited France, Germany, Italy, and Poland.

XVII THE STRANGE STORY OF CATHERINE COOMBES, THE 'GENTLEMAN PAINTER'

THERE are few stranger stories in fiction than that of the life of Catherine Coombes, who, under the name of ' Charley Wilson,' lived and worked as a man for over forty years without her true sex being discovered. She worked at the docks, in a printing office, as a sailor on board ship, and later as a painter and decorator.

One day in October 1897 a little, old, grey-haired man, dressed in a neat suit of clothes, wearing a black bowler hat, and carrying a small bag, walked into the Rochester Row Police Station asking for relief. He told the amazed inspector in charge that he was a woman. He had a quiet pleasant voice, and, although there was nothing that could be called masculine in his face, his figure might have been that of a slight man or woman over sixty years of age. The incredulous inspector sent him on to the relieving officer at Canning Town, and on the Saturday night he presented himself with an order at the West Ham Union. Dressed in the same clothes, he looked a clean, respectable clerk or artisan and was shown to the men's ward.

When ordered to take a bath in the usual way, together with two other applicants for admission, he began to undress ; then he hesitated and asked to see the doctor and matron. The master of the workhouse was sent for, who asked him what was the matter.

The little man replied : ' *I am a woman.*'

The startled master first thought he had to deal with

147

a lunatic, but the man went on to tell him earnestly that his real name was Catherine Coombes, though for forty-two years he had worn men's clothes and passed under the name of ' Charley Wilson.' He was sixty-three years of age and had never revealed his true sex.

The master at once sent for the matron and a nurse who verified his story, and they further discovered that, in the previous July, a Mr. Charley Wilson had fractured his ribs in falling from a scaffold in Surbiton and, although attended by a doctor in Kingston, his sex had never been doubted.

Catherine was then removed to the women's department where she was given the proper outfit, consisting of a blue print-dress and red shawl, which gave her some little trouble before she discovered the proper way to put it on. Thus dressed in women's clothes it was difficult to believe how she could have lived for nearly half a century as a man without detection. Her hair was about two inches long, just turning white, but her eyes were keen and bright and her mouth large and firm.

Later, relating the story of her life, she said she was born at Axbridge in Somersetshire in 1834, and her real name was Catherine Wreford Tozer. She was educated at a girl's college in Cheltenham and, on leaving school at the age of sixteen, married her first cousin, Percival Horatio Coome [or Coombes], who was twenty-three years older than herself. They were married at the Register Office in Cheltenham on 16 October, 1851.

For a time after her marriage she was employed as a schoolmistress and had charge of the Cleeve National School, but owing to her husband's bad treatment of some of the pupils she was obliged to give up her post. He went off to London, and then wrote to her, saying that he had obtained a situation in Chelsea and she had better join him. When she reached Chelsea she found he had no work and had pawned their things, and eventually they had to walk back to Cheltenham. They went to live with Catherine's mother, but soon realizing that he did not intend to keep her, his wife decided to leave him, and she ran off to her brother who lived at Hill-top, West Bromwich.

He took her in, and she helped him as a painter and decorator and so learned his trade. Her husband, however, followed her and persuaded her to open a school at Hazenville. They had not settled there long when he began to ill-treat her and she again left him to return to Hill-top. It was then that she resolved to dress as a man to escape him. Procuring a suit of men's clothes and other outfit, she made them into a parcel and went off to Birmingham, where she took lodgings at a coffee-shop in Snow Hill for her ' brother.' She then managed to make a change of clothes, and doing her own up into a bundle she addressed them to her brother. Having cut off her hair she had all the appearance of a man, and, adopting the name of ' Charley Wilson,' she soon found employment as a house-painter, in which work she was skilled. She left Birmingham for London, where she carried on her trade and became a member of the Painter's Union.

She was known as a good and clean workman and was rarely without a job. She worked for the P. and O. Company for thirteen years and for seven years lived at Camden Terrace, Custom House, where a niece kept house for her, the couple passing as husband and wife until the girl died.

In April 1897 Catherine took lodgings in Railway Terrace, Kingston-on-Thames. She told the landlady that she was a painter and glazier and gave the name of ' Charley Wilson.' She said she had come to work on a job down there, and was a widower and had lost a wife and three children. ' Charley ' used to go off to work every morning and return in the evening with his bag of tools. He was very steady and never late, said his employers. One day when working on a scaffold at Surbiton ' Charley ' fell and broke three ribs. She was carried to her lodgings and was attended by a doctor for three weeks without her true sex being discovered. It was a fact, she said, that she had been attended by half-a-dozen doctors and they had never discovered her secret.

After her accident she obtained a situation as a clerk in a London warehouse. According to Catherine's own statement she never mixed a great deal with other men, and her aloof manner gained her the name among her mates as the ' Gentleman Painter.'

She said : ' I never hesitated to show I disliked coarse and vulgar talk. I earned good wages as a foreman, and never found it necessary to sleep in the same room as a man.'

While in the workhouse, she said to a visitor : ' If I had money I would get out of here in men's clothes and no one would detect me, but at present I cannot work on account of my fractured ribs.'

Catherine Coombe's impersonation, which she kept up successfully for so long, had become second nature with her, and she was never reconciled to living and dressing as a woman for the remainder of her days.

Only once, she declared, was her identity ever discovered, and that was one day early in her career when, dressed as a man, she was painting a pavilion on a Bowling Green at Tewkesbury. On this occasion a man who had known her as ' Mrs. Coombes ' recognized her ; she told him her secret and he made her a promise never to divulge it, which he had faithfully kept.

The story of Catherine Coombes was known to Charles Reade, the dramatist and author of *The Cloister and the Hearth*, who many years ago published a version, different from her own, in the *English Review*.

According to his account, Kate Tozer was the daughter of a carrier, and after leaving school had become a pupil-teacher. She married Tom Coombes, a house-painter, but there was no proof that her husband ill-treated her. Kate is described as a good-looking, eccentric schoolgirl, and there were family quarrels. An aunt died when they were living at Woburn and left her ten pounds. One day, some time later, after being out, she returned to their lodgings dressed in a man's trousers and jacket which she had bought.

' I'm not Kate any longer,' she exclaimed, ' I'm Fred.' Her husband demanded what she meant and she told him that his wages were too small to keep two people, and she intended to double their earnings by working as a painter.

Later, when they moved to Bedford, a girl named Nelly Smith who was apprenticed to a straw-bonnet maker fell in love with ' Fred.' They wrote love-letters to one another, and in the end Nelly eloped with ' Fred.' Her parents were much alarmed when she left them and communicated with the police. They discovered that ' Fred ' came from Woburn and was married. In the meantime, however, Kate, her husband, and Nelly left Bedford together and went to Moulton. The police traced them and broke in on the party, with the girl's father ; they found Tom Coombes seated at a table smoking his pipe, and reading the news, while ' Fred ' and Nelly were reclining on a sofa. Nelly sprang from the sofa and threw her arms round her father's neck, while the police arrested ' Fred ' (still dressed in man's clothes) and took him to Northampton gaol. The case was dropped and he was discharged.

' Kate then pulled her wits together,' says Reade,

' smartened up her male attire and looked a pretty fellow for a maid to pitch her heart on. Her black hair was longish in front, falling on her forehead, but she might easily be mistaken for a boy in his 'teens. She then started her career as " Charley Wilson," the name she took later. She alleged that she went through a form of marriage at Westminster in 1866 and described herself as " Charles Smith," house-painter of Cawston Street, Westminster, while the bride's name was Anne Ridgway.'

The two stories differ so widely, it is evident that Charles Reade was either misinformed or wished to make some picturesque additions to the tale, but there seems little doubt that his ' Kate Tozer ' and ' Catherine Coombes ' were one and the same person.

S OME curious cases of impersonation are brought
to light in the police courts from time to time.
In most of these in which the accused are women
it has been found that they usually assumed men's
clothes as a disguise or for some criminal purpose.
Such cases among men are rarer and there is generally
some physiological reason for the masquerade, and a
medical report is usually called for. The delinquents
are well aware that when once detained by the police
or convicted, the deception is sure to be found out.

About fifty years ago much interest was excited in
the North on the arrest of a young man who for many
years had masqueraded as a woman. His family lived
in a northern town, and when his father died he left
a considerable sum of money to his widow should her
forthcoming child be a daughter. Fate decreed otherwise, and when a son was born the mother decided
to pass the boy off as a girl. She clothed him in girl's
costumes, and he was brought up and educated as a
female and no one was any the wiser. ' She ' became
an active worker in a nonconformist church, and a
Sunday-school teacher. Later, they went to live
in another district, and there ' she ' became engaged
to a young man. A marriage was arranged, but
fortunately the true sex of the ' bride ' was discovered
in time and a warrant was issued for her arrest.

Another strange case was brought to light some
thirty years ago when an inquiry was held into the
death of a person known as ' James Gillson ' who had
led a curious double life. For some years she had lived

in Beresford Street, Camberwell, and afterwards at County Terrace, New Kent Road. Neighbours saw her going about the house in the usual female attire but in the evenings they saw her go out dressed as a man in fashionably cut clothes, wearing a silk hat and a light overcoat over a suit, and accompanied by a small terrier dog. She was a heavy smoker, and had a great fondness for tea, which she drank nearly every hour of the day. When the suspicions of the police were aroused they discovered she had been carrying on frauds all over the country, and had been masquerading for many years in London under ten different names. A warrant was issued for her arrest, and she was being taken to the police-station handcuffed when she suddenly leaped from a tram-car on which she and her escort were travelling and was killed.

A few years ago a girl of twenty-two made her appearance in the dock of the West London Police Court wearing army-breeches, puttees, trench-coat, and a wide-brimmed hat. She was charged with disorderly conduct and had been arrested previously for obtaining money under false pretences, but it was not until she reached Brixton Prison that it was discovered that the supposed young man was a girl.

More recently a young woman of twenty-eight was charged at Oxford with having taken part in raids on costumiers' shops in Slough and Oxford. When she appeared in court she had Eton-cropped hair and was wearing a man's raincoat, flannel trousers, and a sports' jacket. A young man who was charged with her said he employed the girl as a chauffeur and she drove him to the shops.

One witness said he had seen the two men in Slough, one of whom looked very effeminate, but he had looked more effeminate than ever when he jumped to avoid a car.

The police described her as a determined, cunning, and dangerous thief, an inveterate liar, and a menace to the community. She was an associate of thieves and had done no work for the past two years, but had lived on the proceeds of crime. Since July she had paid one firm £177 for the purchase of cars, and she had been convicted five times. With two men she had broken into the shop at Oxford and collected a quantity of goods. They were seen to drive off in a car the number of which was noted. Later, an Uxbridge policeman saw the car and chased it. He jumped on the running-board, but was brushed off as the car was driven against a wall. The woman dressed as a man was driving and eventually the car was overtaken and stopped. The woman was sentenced to four years' penal servitude for shop-breaking, and at her trial the judge remarked ' she had a disastrous record.'

A short time ago a girl of twenty-two appeared at the Thames Police Court wearing a man's trousers with collar and tie. She was charged with breaking two windows in a café.

The police said the girl had told so many stories about herself that they did not know what to believe. She declared that her father had been Mayor of Doncaster for five successive years, and she had received £1170 in damages when her husband had been killed in a motor accident.

After reading a medical report from the prison doctor the magistrate remarked : " It is obvious the kind of life you have been leading."

The girl replied : " I don't think I have been doing any wrong. If you think for a moment I am going to hospital you are mistaken. I'd rather do time. I am only twenty-two, but I can please myself."

Three months with hard labour was the decision of the magistrate in this case, and the girl left the dock with a nonchalant air and her hands in her pockets.

The type of offender, who wears men's clothes as a disguise, is by no means uncommon in our police courts. Quite recently an attractive-looking girl of twenty-five made her appearance in the West Ham Police Court on a charge of stealing ten pounds and certain articles from a ship's officer who had befriended her. She was wearing a grey flannel man's jacket with wide Oxford trousers, a bright red jumper, red silk scarf, and white gloves. She made a statement in which she said she had come out of prison the previous day and had a cheque for ten pounds which no one would cash. The police stated that she had been employed as a singer with a dance band.

While the magistrates were discussing the case the girl began humming tunes, and while singing ' When Irish Eyes are Smiling ' and ' The Girl in the Alice Blue Gown,' she performed some dancing steps in the dock to the amusement of the court. When the chairman of the bench remanded her for further inquiries, she stepped lightly from the dock towards the cells, calling out : " All right, old bean, maybe I'll come and see you again next week."

Cases in which men are found masquerading in feminine clothes are not so frequently met with, but an instance of this kind was brought to light a few months ago, when a man who had been arrested on leaving a cinema theatre dressed as a woman appeared in the dock of a London Police Court. He was wearing a fashionable Persian lamb coat, silk stockings, and high-heeled shoes.

A policewoman who was called as a witness said " she sat behind the person and followed him to the women's cloak-room on the first floor and then to the cloak-room on the ground floor. A police sergeant stated when he arrested the man he was wearing a wig, a woman's hat and gloves, silk underclothes, ear-rings in his ears, a silver-fox fur round his neck, and carried a hand-bag. There were rings on his fingers and a bracelet on his arm. His lips were rouged, there was make-up on his face, and he had false eyelashes.

This man was remanded for a medical report and was later bound over.

These few instances of impersonation in modern times serve to show that this curious phase of human abnormality still exists and has never been eradicated.

PART TWO

Men who Impersonated Women

EFFEMINACY as regards dress was not unusual
at the Court of Louis XIV, and even Philip,
Duke of Orleans, who became the husband of
' Minette,' the favourite sister of King Charles II, was
among those who loved to array themselves in women's
clothes.

There seems to have been no motive for his
peculiarity beyond vanity of an inordinate character,
for he was never a sexual pervert, but the craze for
posturing as a girl continued throughout his life.
Saint-Simon described him as ' a little pot-bellied man,
mounted on such high heels that they were more
like stilts. He always dressed as a woman and was
covered with rings, bracelets, and precious stones
everywhere. He wore a long wig, black and
powdered, and ribbons wherever they could be placed.
He was redolent of all kinds of perfumery and accused
of putting on an imperceptible touch of rouge.'

Madame de la Fayette, who was one of the trusted
friends of the Princess Henrietta Anne and had many
opportunities of seeing him, tells us that all his
inclinations were towards feminine occupations. She
says : ' He was handsome but of a beauty more
suitable to a princess than a prince. Even his wife
mentions his love for finery and noted the care he
bestowed on his complexion. He is interested in
needlework and dances, but dances like a woman.'

The Princess Palatine, whom he married after the
sudden death of Henrietta Anne, says : ' He had the
manners of a woman rather than those of a man.

He liked to chat, play, eat well, and perform his toilet, in short everything that women love. He delighted to be with women and young girls, to attire them, and dress their hair.'

Abbé de Choisy, whose father was the Duke's Chancellor and who later developed a similar peculiarity, says in referring to Philip : ' I was dressed up as a girl every time he came to the house. He wore an embroidered bodice tight to the waist. They took off his coat and put on him a woman's mantle and petticoats. When he was dressed and decked out we played " rimo," the fashionable game at the time.'

THE MAN-WIFE
(From a print of the eighteenth century.)

PHILIP, DUKE OF ORLEANS
(After the painting by Wallerant-Vaillant, 1623–1677.)

A CURIOUS reason has been suggested to explain why certain ecclesiastics in the past may have become obsessed with the idea of dressing in feminine attire ; it is that certain vestments used in the priesthood had their origin in the garments worn by women. Their richness of decoration and colour appealed to the æsthetic side of their characters. This æsthetic attraction has a distinctive and marked effect on the sexes, and the love of adornment in bright clothing and sparkling objects may be said to be the offspring of vanity and sexual instincts.

The average man as a rule shuns showy garb, while the woman delights in colour, ornaments, and decorative clothing.

Among the instances of the strange infatuation for dressing in female attire among ecclesiastics, was that of the Abbé de Choisy, who was well known at the Court of Louis XIV.

François Timoléon de Choisy was born in Paris on 16 August 1644, and was the youngest of a family of three brothers and two sisters. His father was Chancellor to the Duke of Orleans. His mother had reached the age of forty-three when he was born. She idolized him as a child and from babyhood regarded him as a girl and dressed him accordingly. The craze for wearing feminine garments continued during his youth, and up to the age of eighteen he wore no other costumes. Owing to the position of his family, he was received in the highest class of society in Paris, and no one appears to have taken any objection to his peculiarity ; on the contrary, young girls copied the style in which his hair was dressed, and fashionable ladies copied his elaborate toilettes.

' Although a male,' says a writer of the time, ' he was the most charming female in the world. He possessed all the attractions of a very pretty woman and dressed like a thorough coquette.'

Although he soon betrayed a tendency to lead a wild life, he responded to the wishes of his family to enter the Church, and on the recommendation of the Archbishop of Paris was received as an Abbé without opposition.

Before this, at the age of eighteen, he developed a passion for the stage, and made his first appearance at a theatre in Bordeaux. At that time he dressed completely as a girl, with a waist encircled by tight-fitting corsets which made his hips and breast more prominent.

' During five months,' he tells us in his *Memoirs*, ' I played in comedy at the theatre dressed as a girl. Everybody was deceived and I had lovers, but was very discreet and had a reputation for prudence and virtue.'

He thus describes himself and his clothes at the period before he entered the Church : ' I had a bodice embroidered with natural flowers on a silver ground, and a skirt of the same material with a long train. The skirt was fastened up on both sides with yellow and silver ribbons. The bodice was very high and padded out to make it appear that I had a bust, and as a matter of fact I had as much as a girl of fifteen.'

He seems delighted to tell of his feminine vanities and goes on to say : ' From my childhood my mother had made me wear bodices that were extremely tight, and this had pushed up the flesh, which was fat and plump. I also took care of my neck, rubbing it every night with veal broth and a pomade of sheep's-foot oil which makes the skin soft and white.

' My black hair was done into large curls. I had big

diamond ear-rings, a dozen patches, and a necklace of false pearls. I exchanged at Paris my diamond cross for five ornamental pins that I placed in my hair, which I also decorated with yellow and silver ribbons. A large mask covered both cheeks to prevent sunburn, for it was June, and I had white gloves and a fan.'

It was in this array De Choisy went to a garden fête.

His bedroom, we are told, was equipped with everything dear to the feminine heart, with lace-edged sheets and pillows tied up with flame-coloured ribbons.

After he had taken Holy Orders he had his ears pierced and wore embroidered bodices and a black and gold dressing-gown trimmed with white satin. He still wore patches and a little cap with a top-knot of ribbon.

' I did not wear small clothes as they did not seem to me to be feminine,' he says, and he later observes : ' I thought myself really and truly a woman.'

De Choisy delighted to play the part of mistress of his house and gives us a picture of how he entertained Madame Dupois, her daughters, and some other ladies he had invited to see him.

' I was well got-up on that occasion,' he tells us. ' I had on a dress of white damask lined with black taffeta, a train half an ell long, a bodice of black _moiré_ trimmed with silver and surmounted with a large bow of black ribbon over which hung a muslin cravat with tassels, a skirt of black velvet, and underneath two white petticoats. I had well-powdered pinks and twelve or fifteen patches.

' When the _curé_ came, he exclaimed, " Ah, Madame, you are splendidly dressed. Are you going to a ball ? " " No, Monsieur," I replied, " I am giving a supper to my fair neighbours." '

All the talk was about fashions, and when the guests were leaving he allowed the women to kiss him.

At that time he was living in the Faubourg St. Marceau and kept up a large establishment with many servants and had a clever lady's maid to dress and look after him.

It was well known that he kept a mistress secluded in the house who was known as ' Madame de Sancy,' but she rarely made an appearance.

Nothing appeared to give him greater delight than to be dressed and decorated by his maid, who used to powder and patch him with meticulous care, arranging his hair in the style he affected. Among the neighbours who used to visit him was a lady named Mademoiselle Charlotte, who fell in love with him, and at a party one evening she appeared, to his great delight, clad as a boy. He was so pleased with the transformation and how charming they looked together, that he commissioned M. de Troyes to paint their portraits. His next idea was to have what he called a ' marriage of conscience,' and to this end invited all Charlotte's family to a fête. Before supper was announced, the guests witnessed a mock ceremony of marriage between Choisy and Charlotte, who impersonated the bridegroom.

This came to the ears of the Cardinal of Paris, who sent an emissary to make inquiries. He was received by the Abbé and entertained with great friendliness. In the end he said he would tell His Eminence that the costume worn by Choisy was fit and proper and that all the story reported was slanderous.

Nevertheless, Charlotte took up her residence at the house in the Faubourg St. Marceau, where she was known as Monsieur de Maulny. Choisy says in his *Memoirs*, in relating this incident : ' Monsieur de Maulny had, at my request, had his hair cut short like a man's and on the wedding night wore a dressing-gown, a night-cap and flame-coloured ribbons in his hair.'

Eventually, after some months, they got tired of one another, and Charlotte's parents having found a suitable man, who was a wood-turner by trade, to become her husband, she resolved to resume her female garb once more and Choisy gave her up.

After this, for a time, he dressed in man's clothes and developed a mania for gambling, at which he lost large sums of money. First, his diamond ear-rings went, and in the end he had to sell his house. On the death of his mother, however, he came into 70,000 francs, 2000 of which he at once spent on another pair of diamond ear-rings, but he had enough left to adorn himself with splendid costumes.

'Happy should I have been,' he writes, 'if I had always played the part of a woman even if I had been ugly.' So he resumed his female attire and had his portrait painted by Ferdonad, a famous artist at the time.

When he was thirty-two years old much amusement was caused in Paris when it was announced that the Abbé Choisy had been appointed to the suite of the ambassador whom Louis XIV had decided to send to the King of Siam. The chief of the expedition was the Chevalier de Chaumont, and the party sailed from Brest on 3 May 1685.

The Abbé was very sea-sick during the voyage, which lasted four months, but eventually they arrived in Siam in safety. Choisy kept a diary of the journey and occupied himself by studying Siamese, but the mission only remained in the country for three months. During this time the Abbé became very devout and preached to the crew of the ship on which they returned, but he is said to have always expressed a regret when he talked of 'the delightful time when his waist was tightly compressed into a corset, his breast uncovered and his long curls falling artfully over his shoulders.'

He was an adept in the art of flattery, and on his return to Paris he endeavoured to ingratiate himself with the King to obtain his Royal favour. He busied himself with writing books, one being *A Life of David* which he dedicated to Louis XIV, and the other *A Journal of a Voyage to Siam*.

He had played the part of a woman so long, however, that it had become second nature to him, so it is with little wonder we read that in the privacy of the apartment he occupied in the Luxembourg, skirts, petticoats, and feminine finery again made their appearance, although he no longer dared to wear them in public.

He had now reached the age of seventy, and although he had to assume male attire, even in his old age in the seclusion of his study, he loved to wear some of the faded female finery which reminded him of the past. A few years later his health began to fail, but he lived to reach the age of eighty-one and died in Paris in 1724.

In endeavouring to throw some light on the motive for his curious eccentricities, in his *Memoirs* he says : ' I have tried to find out how the strange idea came to me of believing myself a woman. It is an attribute of God to be loved and adored and man—so far as his weak nature will permit—has the same ambition. It is beauty which creates love and beauty is generally woman's portion ; when it happens that men have or believe they have attractions for which they may be loved, they try to increase them by putting on women's attire. Then they feel the inexpressible pleasure of being loved. I have had that pleasant experience many a time when I have been at a ball or a theatre in a beautiful dress with patches and diamonds and when I have heard someone whisper near me : " There is a pretty woman ! " I have felt a pleasure so great that it is beyond all comparison.'

This candid statement or confession shows that an

overweening vanity was among the dominating influences of his life. This, together with the desire of his mother in early life for a female child, to satisfy which she dressed the boy in girl's clothes, strongly affected him as he grew to the age of puberty. Even later, when he knew that he was not in reality a woman, he still aped a woman's manners, speech, and habits. He knew he was but acting a part as he did in early life on the stage.

THE story and career of a young Frenchman who was so convinced that he should have been of the opposite sex that he assumed the dress of a woman throughout his life, was brought to light in 1735 through a dispute over his will.

His name was Pierre Aymon du Moret, and he was the youngest son of a barrister of that name practising in Toulouse. His mother was devoted to him and watched over his childhood and after-training with the tenderest care, but she died before he reached manhood. During her life he never mixed with other boys of his own age and hardly ever left the house, but preferred to be with her or to be alone. After his mother's death, his father, with whom he never appears to have agreed very well, became dissatisfied with his solitary way of living, though he never reproached him for his peculiar habits.

It was noticed by friends who came to the house that young Pierre Aymon was becoming vain respecting his appearance, and was frequently seen gazing at his face in a mirror. About this time a lady living at Toulouse wished to find a young man as a tutor for her two sons, and hearing that Pierre Aymon du Moret was seeking such a post she asked him to call upon her. After an interview, pleased with his manner and appearance, the lady decided to engage him, especially as he told her that he had devoted himself to the study of theology and law and recently had obtained his degree.

It was not long after he had taken up his duties when it was noticed in the house that his ways and manners were very effeminate, and were more like those of a woman than a man. He frequently blushed when anything was said to offend his susceptibilities and he was very vain.

One day, when his employer returned home unexpectedly, to her utter amazement she surprised her boys' tutor, arrayed in one of her dresses and admiring himself before a mirror. He blushed crimson and was much confused when asked the reason for his strange conduct. In explanation he told the astounded lady that he was in reality a woman. He further declared that for certain private reasons, on which the preservation of his family's property depended, he had been forced to dress as a man, but as soon as the time arrived he would revert to his true sex and no harm would have been done. His employer, however, was by no means satisfied with this explanation and after accusing him with deceiving her, discharged him at once.

The affair soon became known and talked about in the town, for no one would believe that the young tutor whom they had seen with his pupils was a girl and not a man. He admitted that he had become obsessed with the idea that Nature had intended him to be a woman and so was firmly convinced that he was of the female sex. It transpired that his mother tried to destroy this impression which had been apparent in his youth, but on her death he was left without her influence. His father allowed him to grow up in his own way, and while Pierre became a theological student at his own wish, he spent all his money in buying girls' clothes. He even bought materials to cut out and make women's costumes in his rooms, and had the greatest delight, when he had finished a dress, in putting it on and admiring himself standing before a mirror.

Unable to obtain a further post as tutor in Toulouse, he left the town and went to live at Bagnères. There he assumed female dress altogether and was immensely proud when he succeeded in converting other people to his belief that he was a woman. At length, his father heard of this masquerading, recalled him and reminded him of his duty as a son ; he demanded that he should help him in his office and at the courts. In response, Pierre informed him that it was not moral or proper for a girl to work in a lawyer's office, and he ought to be employed in dressmaking or sewing. His father was greatly enraged at this answer and, losing all patience, threatened to employ measures of the utmost severity against him if he did not obey his orders. To this Pierre returned an insolent answer and his father, determined to have nothing further to do with him, forbade him the house.

Peace had not been made between them when M. du Moret died and Pierre's relations, including his elder brother, used every effort to convince him of his errors and entreated him to return to his home. But all in vain ; he would not listen to their advice, and continued to promenade the streets dressed in women's clothes though he was often jeered at by boys who ran after him.

He continued to act in this manner for years until he reached the age of forty, when he bought a little farm in the country and gave up wearing the attire of a female for a time. His craze now entered on a fresh phase and he began to dress himself as a child. The reason for this change he gave out was, that he now wished to repair the injury he had done to his parents in his youth and had therefore adopted the ' clothes of innocence.'

He now called himself ' Mademoiselle Rosette ' and gave all his time to feminine pursuits and religious exercises. He became very devout, never missed Mass, went regularly to confession, and took the sacrament. But these ardent devotions did not prevent him spending hours over his toilet and dressing. He would stand before his mirror for hours at a time and lock himself in a room in order to contemplate his person. He squeezed his bust into steel stays to give it grace and fullness, and used every conceivable method to mould his shape to resemble that of a woman.

There was one thing, however, which he was never able to overcome—the growth of hair on his face. In spite of daily use of pumice-stone and tweezers, to his chagrin the hair was still apparent, for his beard was a strong one and would grow ; furthermore, it grew a long way down his cheeks. He used to employ the greater part of the day in trying to conceal it by means of paint, and when he thought himself presentable would set out to pay visits anywhere he knew he would be received as ' Mademoiselle Rosette.'

Gossip and unpleasant stories naturally began to circulate in the neighbourhood in which he lived and people began to avoid him. He then resolved to leave his farm and removed to Cahors, but there also matters grew unpleasant and in a short time he returned to Bagnères.

After the death of his father, Pierre having refused to come forward and claim his share of the property, his elder brother, Jean du Moret, took possession of the whole of the estate. Someone now urged Pierre to assert his rights and he brought an action against his brother which resulted in his favour, and an arrangement was made for him to receive a regular allowance from the property.

This addition to his fortune provided him with more money for dress and he at once ordered a number of extravagant costumes in which he delighted to appear in the streets of the town and in church. At length these eccentricities began to be noticed by the local authorities, but they had no power to interfere with him so long as he kept within the law.

In May 1725, ' Mademoiselle Rosette ' was suddenly taken very ill and the doctor who was called in, well aware of his peculiar way of living, took the opportunity while he was in a fainting attack to examine him. To his amazement, he discovered the entire body of his patient to be tightly sewn up in leather ; in this way the wretched man, while enduring the most dreadful torture, had tried to carry out his deception. The doctor immediately cut all the leather sheathing away and threw it out of the room. When Pierre recovered consciousness and saw what had happened he flew into a fury, jumped up, hit out at the doctor, and fought all who approached him.

Later, when he found his women's dresses had also disappeared, his anger knew no bounds ; he was completely distraught, and eventually they were given back to him. When he had recovered from this attack, ' Mademoiselle Rosette ' again made her appearance in public in costumes of the latest style.

He removed from the house where these events had taken place and shortly afterwards, on the death of his elder brother, came in for a considerable fortune.

Certain unscrupulous priests who knew him are said to have used their influence and got him to make a will from which they would benefit. He made such a will, excluding all his heirs without hesitation, and duly signed it. His health again failed at this time and he was removed to a hospital where he died, still wearing the underclothes of a woman.

The Syndic of the institution in which he died took possession of his property, but when his legal heirs heard of his death they demanded the annulment of the will on the grounds that he was not in his right mind when it was executed.

There can be little doubt that Pierre Aymon du Moret was a monomaniac and this view was held by the authorities, for on 30 April, 1735, an Order in Council decreed the nullity of the will and ordered the refundment of his property to the natural heirs.

AMONG other eccentric clerical *poseurs* of the early eighteenth century was the Abbé d'Entragues, who is said to have been related to the de Balzac family. Like others, his feminine predilections appear to have been influenced by his early environment. It is stated that his mother had a great desire for a daughter and, keenly disappointed when her baby turned out to be a boy, she resolved to bring him up as a girl. As a child he was dressed and treated as a girl, and when he reached the age of adolescence his complexion was kept pale by frequent bleeding. At night he wore girl's attire and donned ' a woman's nightcap trimmed with lace, a top-knot, a corset laced with ribbons, a bedgown, and patches.'

He became a great wit and later when he entered the Church and was made an abbé, he wore in the daytime the regulation clerical attire of his calling. However, he soon got tired of the vows the Church imposed upon him and embraced the Protestant faith. For this recantation he was exiled from the country, but later on, when he was able to return to Paris, he repented and again rejoined the Roman Catholic Church. At the same time he resumed his former eccentricities and used to don full feminine evening dress whenever an opportunity occurred.

He mixed in good society where his gift of conversation and witty speeches made him a universal favourite, but his rather caustic humour sometimes annoyed his listeners and made him enemies. Among his circle was the Princess de Conti, as he always strove to shine in the society of great ladies and intrigue them by his mischievous *mots*.

He is described as a tall, well-made man of singular pallor which he constantly maintained by being regularly bled by his apothecary, whom he was wont to call his ' dainty.' He slept with his arms fastened above his head in order to keep his hands white. Even in his clerical costume he often appeared fantastic owing to little feminine vanities he affected.

When he was exiled, more on account of the profligate life he led than for his defection from the Church, he went to Caen and was there visited by Monsieur Pelletier de Sonce.

Saint-Simon, in his account of this visit, says that Pelletier found him in ' a nice clean bedroom with a nice clean bed in it, open on all sides. In the bed was a person sitting up and doing tapestry work, elegantly dressed, wearing a woman's nightcap trimmed with lace, top-knot and other finery, a corset laced with ribbons, and a bedgown, while his face was covered with patches. At first sight Pelletier drew back, thinking he had entered the bedroom of some woman of easy virtue. Murmuring some excuses he was about to gain the door close behind him when the person in the bed called him and begged him to approach, then gave him his hand and began to laugh.

' It was Abbé d'Entragues,' he says, ' who generally sleeps in a garb of this sort, but always in a woman's nightcap more or less decorated.'

After his return to Paris to become a Protestant he soon got into trouble again, for he had given out that he was being persecuted and had gone to the chaplain of the Dutch Ambassador to make his abjuration of the Roman Catholic faith.

One Christmas Eve he paid a visit to a lady who had invited him to accompany her to midnight Mass.

" I shall never go to Mass again all my life," he exclaimed. His hostess and others present were greatly surprised at this declaration, and someone asked him why.

" Since I have had the happiness to take the Communion of both kinds with six hundred of my brothers, I am resolved never to go to Mass again," he calmly replied.

This statement naturally set all Paris talking and the matter was discussed at a meeting of priests called by the Bishop. It was suggested that he should be arrested and sent to the Bastille, but before this threat could be put into operation, he escaped and fled to Lille, where he sent in his name to the Commandant of the town.

The Duchess of Orleans, the Regent's mother, who was friendly towards him, refers to this in a letter she wrote on 11 January 1720 : ' I think the Abbé d'Entragues has become quite mad. I wrote to you that he had followed the advice I gave him, and had fled and arrived in Flanders. He was close to Tournai where he would have been safe, but instead of going there he went to Lille where he remained several days. As no one knew him there he would have run no risk if he had stayed quiet, but on the contrary, he must show himself in public places, he must like a Jew exchange bank-notes and inveigh against my son to the Government.

' The Commandant of Lille was informed of this and had him arrested, and it was discovered that he was the Abbé d'Entragues. Did you ever hear of such madness ? My son did all he could to save him ; he gave him time to get away and did not have him pursued ; but then this idiot goes and speaks against him in a public place.'

Although imprisoned in the fortress at Lille, d'Entragues was treated very leniently and given all he wanted, even to the dolls which he played with like a child.

After being detained a few months he was allowed to return to Paris, where to show his penitence he was a constant attendant at his old church and appeared at Mass carrying a huge breviary. His old passion for feminine clothes still continued and he loved to appear in full dress as if he was going to a ball.

This strange man lived to the age of eighty, and at the end it was said of him that ' he finished in a very Christian manner a life which had not been very Christian.'

ALTHOUGH volumes have been written concerning d'Eon de Beaumont, well known as the Chevalier d'Eon, no account of notorious impersonators would be complete without some mention of his strange and adventurous career. The controversy concerning his sex, which he changed more than once, lasted for nearly half a century, and the mystery was not solved until his death in 1810.

Charles Geneviève Louis André Timothée d'Eon de Beaumont was born at Tonnerre in France on 5 October 1728. His father was Louis d'Eon de Beaumont, who held the post of director of the King's demesnes and was a man of some position.

Until he reached the age of twelve, young d'Eon received instruction from the Abbé Marcenay, curé of the Church of St. Peter, but afterwards he was sent to Paris to complete his education at the Collège Mazarin, where he graduated as Doctor of Civil and Canon Law. He was called to the Bar of the Parliament and obtained the post of secretary to M. Bertier de Sauvigny, who at that time was Intendant of the district of Paris.

As a young man he is described as being short in height with a slight, girlish figure, and effeminate in appearance. His favourite recreation was fencing, in which he became highly proficient and soon attained a reputation for his skill with the rapier.

Through his connexion with de Sauvigny, he became known to the Prince de Conti, who recommended him to Louis XV as a suitable person to accompany the

Chevalier Douglas, who was about to be sent to Russia by the King on a secret and confidential mission. The object of the journey was said to be to gain the support and influence of the Russian Government to place the Prince de Conti on the throne of Poland.

To avoid publicity it was thought desirable for them to enter the country secretly as ordinary travellers, and so Douglas and his companion set out for Russia and arrived at St. Petersburg in 1755.

According to one account, Douglas, taking advantage of d'Eon's girlish appearance and figure, persuaded him to assume feminine attire and in this guise introduced him at the Russian Court as his niece. Dressed as a woman he is thus said to have freely enjoyed the society of the maids-of-honour, and succeeded in presenting the Czarina with a private autograph letter from Louis XV, explaining the object of their visit, but this like many other stories about him has been proved to be fictitious.

However, he became appointed as secretary to the French Embassy at St. Petersburg and afterwards was entrusted with some confidential dispatches which had to be taken to Paris. He started on the journey, but on reaching Vienna heard the news of the Austrian victory over the King of Prussia at Prague, and realizing its importance, he at once took horse and rode off at great speed to Paris. Although he is said to have been thrown and broken his leg on the journey, he was the first to bring the news to King Louis, who was so pleased that he gave him a gold snuff-box and a commission as a lieutenant in the dragoons.

D'Eon's foot was now on the ladder to success; he gained the favour of powerful friends and through their influence was again sent to Russia as secretary to l'Hôpital, who was acting as the intermediary in the secret correspondence that was then passing between King Louis and the Czarina.

THE CHEVALIER D'EON AT THE AGE OF TWENTY-FIVE
(From a painting by Angelica Kauffman after Latour.)

THE CHEVALIER D'EON AT THE AGE OF THIRTY-SIX
(From a mezzotint by Vispré.)

In 1760, d'Eon had a serious illness and received permission to return to France, where on his arrival, he developed smallpox, which incapacitated him for some months. After his recovery at the end of that year the King granted him an annual pension of 2000 livres and he was given permission to join the Army as aide-de-camp to the Marshal and the Count de Broglie, with whom he saw service in the field.

When the Duke de Nivernais was appointed Ambassador to the Court of St. James, he nominated d'Eon as his first secretary and with a numerous suite they set out for England and landed at Dover. Continuing their journey to Canterbury, they decided to stay the night at the Red Lion Inn, where they were received with great honour by the host, who, determining to make the best of a good opportunity, presented the secretary next morning with a bill for £44 10s. 8d., which had to be paid with a good grace.

The new Ambassador was commissioned by his government to carry on negotiations with respect to the so-called Treaty of Paris, and certain terms having been found which required modification, d'Eon was chosen by the English Ministers to carry the dispatches to Paris. On his arrival, he was received very graciously by the King, who awarded him 6000 livres from the privy purse and conferred on him the Order of St. Louis and the title of Chevalier.

The Chevalier d'Eon soon became a social celebrity in Paris, and with money at his command, cut a figure in Court society. He was introduced to the Duchess de Nivernais and the Countess de Rochefort (with whom he became a special favourite) and to many of the great ladies at Court.

On the withdrawal of the Duke de Nivernais from London the Count Guerchy, a man whom d'Eon greatly disliked, was suggested as Ambassador in his place. In the meantime d'Eon was promoted to be

French Resident and Chargé d'Affaires and was again prominent in London. After the departure of de Nivernais he began to play the part of an ambassador and entertained largely such distinguished visitors as Lalande and la Condamine. As Minister Plenipotentiary he was received on an equal footing with ambassadors of the highest standing. He was welcomed at the Court of St. James by Lord Hertford and Lord March, and he found favour with King George III and Queen Charlotte.

It was about this time that Louis became obsessed with a desire to invade England, an ambition which was unknown to some of his Ministers. The King's idea, however, was apparently known to d'Eon, as Broglie cautioned and instructed him ' to be very careful and keep a watch on his papers.' Even Count Guerchy, the newly-appointed ambassador, was not entrusted with the secret. Louis, however, evidently trusted d'Eon implicitly, for on 3 June 1763, he wrote urging him to observe ' the greatest secrecy ' and sent him a special cypher for communications.

Thus, while the Chevalier was being received at St. James as ambassador, he was actually a secret agent of France and was cognizant of a plot for the invasion of Britain, a fact which it is important to remember in connexion with the events which followed.

The French Embassy at that time was located in Soho Square and here d'Eon awaited the arrival of Guerchy, the new ambassador. Before he arrived in London, however, d'Eon, according to his own statement, received the following letter from King Louis :

' VERSAILLES,
' 4 October 1763.

' You have served me as usefully in woman's clothes as in those which you now wear.

' Resume them at once and withdraw into the

city. I warn you that the King this day signed, but only with the stamp and not with his hand, an order for your return to France. But I command you to remain in England with all your papers until I send you further instructions. You are not in safety at your residence and here you would find powerful enemies.

'LOUIS.'

The authenticity of this cryptic letter has been long denied, although d'Eon always declared he received and acted on it. It is obvious from the first paragraph that d'Eon had been using women's clothes as a disguise. That he had done so previously is shown by his portrait dressed as a woman which is said to have been painted by Latour in 1753.

Count Guerchy duly arrived in London and handed to d'Eon letters of recall, instructing him to present them to King George without delay. He told him he was to proceed to Paris at once but he was not to appear at Court until he was told to do so. D'Eon began to pack up his effects, but he decided to retain a number of confidential and official papers as well as all the private documents and correspondence with King Louis relating to the proposed invasion of England.

On hearing of this Guerchy demanded that he should hand over all the papers to him, but d'Eon replied that he had only kept the documents he considered he had a right to keep. This dispute gave rise to considerable ill-feeling and led to frequent altercations between them.

A few days later d'Eon went to dine at the French Embassy, and soon after dinner he appeared to become extremely drowsy and complained of feeling unwell. He returned to his lodgings on foot, where he fell asleep in his chair and when aroused declared he felt 'as if his stomach was on fire.' After he had recovered he asserted that Guerchy had caused opium to be put in his wine, so that while under the influence of the drug he might ' be put in a sedan-chair, carried to the Thames and put on a vessel and taken to France.' Guerchy, on that evening, was dining with the Earl of Sandwich and was not at the Embassy when d'Eon was there, but according to the Chevalier's account the Ambassador had instructed a physician, whom he kept in his house, to place opium in his wine, and he declared he was sure that he had narrowly escaped foul play.

D'Eon, now convinced that his lodging was being watched, removed his belongings and went to live with a friend called La Rozière who resided at 38 Brewer Street, at that time a fashionable part of town.

Guerchy, now angry at his failure to get possession of the secret documents, applied and got an order from King Louis demanding d'Eon's extradition. French police officers were sent from Paris to apprehend the Chevalier, but the British Government would not allow this arrest or the seizure of his papers ; on hearing this, Guerchy tried to arrange for the Frenchmen to kidnap d'Eon privately and put him on board a ship at Gravesend bound for France.

Being informed of this plot, d'Eon barricaded himself in at his lodgings at Brewer Street, where it is said ' he kept a lamp burning throughout the night and had a red-hot poker by his side during the day.'

In the basement of the house he lodged several ex-dragoons of his old regiment and some deserters he had picked up in London. He enlisted them in his service and armed them with ' four brace of pistols, two guns, and eight sabres.' Thus prepared for any emergency he awaited events ; but nothing happened.

A little later he received an unexpected blow, when a notice appeared in the *London Gazette* stating that

His Majesty King George III had forbidden the Chevalier d'Eon his Court, and that the French Government had formally divested him of all diplomatic status, pronounced him guilty of High Treason, and declared that all his arrears of emoluments were forfeited to the Crown.

Thus, deprived of his post and without means, d'Eon began a bitter pamphleteering campaign against Guerchy and published several important letters to discredit him. The British authorities were aware that d'Eon was in possession of a quantity of secret documents which they could not afford to have disclosed, and they are said to have offered him £20,000 for them.

' The leaders of the English Opposition,' he says, ' have offered me any money I may require on consideration that I deliver them my papers and letters.'

King Louis became alarmed about the precious documents in the Chevalier's possession. Afraid that they might fall into the hands of the British Government he decided to try a policy of conciliation, and to this end he dispatched the Chevalier de Nort, one of Broglie's secretaries, to London to see if he could arrange the matter. Before de Nort left Paris, Choiseul suggested as an attractive bait that d'Eon should be offered employment in the French Army, but it was agreed that de Nort should first try to purchase the documents.

On his arrival in London, de Nort called on the Chevalier in Brewer Street and opened negotiations by offering him a small sum of money for the papers, but d'Eon said he could not surrender them because Guerchy had instituted proceedings against him for libel.

It appears that Guerchy, stung by d'Eon's action in publishing letters which charged him with having attempted to drug him, had already applied for a writ and had engaged a man to write a refutation of d'Eon's allegations. The Chevalier, on meeting this individual in the Green Park one afternoon, took him by the collar and gave him a sound thrashing with his cane. After this, fearing reprisals, d'Eon never left his lodgings without being accompanied by two or three of his friends as a bodyguard. ' We have sham fights every day,' he wrote. ' At night-time we make reconnaissance at Ranelagh and Vauxhall. I am always at the head of my little force.'

Meanwhile the libel action brought by Guerchy against d'Eon came on for trial. The Chevalier did not put in an appearance but was found guilty in his absence and sentence was postponed.

Shortly afterwards two officers of the Court were sent to d'Eon's house in Brewer Street to notify him officially of the verdict, but on arrival they found he had disappeared and his whereabouts were unknown. They traced him to a house of a Mrs. Eddowes and, armed with a warrant, ' they burst open the doors and cupboards and even the valises in their search for me,' says d'Eon, ' but they only found my cousin quietly warming himself by the fire with Mrs. Eddowes and another lady. *This lady* was she who is generally called the Chevalier d'Eon.'

D'Eon then took refuge in the house of a Madame Dufour, who subsequently declared that during the three months he stayed with her he always dressed as a female. Here he was visited by Treyssac de Vergy, who stated he had come to England with the promise of being appointed on the Embassy staff in the Chevalier's place and had called there before d'Eon left.

He now assured d'Eon that he had been hired to poison him, and failing that to assassinate him, at the instance of the Marshal and the Count de Broglie. He also made serious charges against Guerchy, and d'Eon, delighted to get someone to support his allegations against the ambassador, on 12 February 1765 applied for the indictment of Guerchy on a charge of ' Having maliciously solicited de Vergy to kill and murder d'Eon de Beaumont.'

This was granted and the Grand Jury meeting at the Old Bailey on 1 March found ' a true bill against the Comte de Guerchy for conspiracy against the life of d'Eon de Beaumont.'

The news of this action caused a great sensation both in Paris and in London and further interest was excited by the report that one Chazal, Guerchy's butler, and who was said to have been instrumental in administering the poison, had taken flight and disappeared.

Guerchy, however, refused to accept the jurisdiction of any English court, although he was summoned several times to appear at Lincoln's Inn. The case was apparently allowed to collapse and in the end was definitely withdrawn.

King Louis, still alarmed about the fate of his secret correspondence, then instructed the Count de Broglie to write to d'Eon informing him that if he would forget the past he would prevail on the King to grant him a pension and he would also be again entrusted with any secret correspondence between Paris and London. This letter is said to have been accompanied by a private autograph letter from the King himself. On receipt of this d'Eon decided to consider Broglie's proposal, and the way was smoothed by the recall of the Comte de Guerchy as ambassador from London.

His successor was M. Durand, a man who was friendly to the Chevalier, and soon after he arrived to take up his post, he managed to persuade d'Eon to part with one of the more important papers the King wished to recover. In return for this, d'Eon received another Royal letter containing the promise of a reward for his services in Russia, together with a pension of 12,000 livres a year.

On 13 June 1765, d'Eon was outlawed by judgment of the Coroners of Middlesex for not surrendering himself to receive the sentence in Guerchy's action for libel against him ; but this did not disconcert the Chevalier, and he settled down to enjoy life in London, where he had made many friends. He took apartments in Petty France, Westminster, and occupied his time in writing political and other essays which he published under the title of *Les Loisirs du Chevalier d'Eon*.

About this time he was introduced to Earl Ferrars and they became so friendly that he was frequently invited to stay at Staunton Harold, the Earl's country residence. Being hard up, d'Eon obtained a loan from the Earl and in 1770 gave him as security the secret papers which he had so long guarded. The Chevalier was now often seen in Society, and owing to his attractive personality combined with the romance which surrounded his career, he became very popular. He was a favourite with both sexes and it is said that ' several wealthy ladies of good families set their caps at the fascinating Chevalier, but he showed himself indifferent to their charms and was more partial to his friends of the male sex.'

Rumours now began to circulate that d'Eon was a woman and that he had been seen dressed in feminine clothes. The Comte du Châtelet, who had succeded Durand as ambassador, is said to have stated he was convinced that the Chevalier was a female, and the matter soon became a topic of discussion in the clubs. Opinions differed and wagers began to be made as to d'Eon's real sex and whether he was a man or a woman.

Princess Daschkov, who was staying in London at this time, is said to have revived the story of d'Eon's escapades with the maids-of-honour at St. Petersburg, which lent further colour to the gossip. At White's and Almack's bets were freely made and taken and in 1770 some venturesome person actually began to issue gambling policies of insurance on the Chevalier's sex.

He is described by Angelo at this time as being ' rather effeminate in appearance, with blue eyes, pale complexion, and a dark beard,' from which many began to assume he was a ' bearded woman.'

D'Eon became intensely annoyed at this gossip and the reports of betting on his sex. He retaliated by thrashing several of the offenders, but in spite of his repeated denials that he was of the female sex, and of a sworn affidavit, the betting continued. The frequent repetition of these rumours led some people to believe in them, and d'Eon began to receive offers of considerable sums of money if he would reveal his true sex.

The Comte de Broglie's secretary Drouet, who had been on a mission to London, returned to Paris and informed the King that the ' Sieur d'Eon *is a woman* and nothing but *a woman,* of whom he has all the attributes.' He said that d'Eon had begged him to keep the secret. This statement naturally surprised both King Louis and Broglie and they could not believe it.

After the death of the King a great longing came on d'Eon to return to his native land, and he sent an appeal to Broglie asking for permission to return. In 1774, in response to this, the Marquis de Prunevaux was sent to London with the object of reopening negotiations with d'Eon. He was empowered to promise him the continuance of his annuity, the restoration of his military rank, and a safe conduct to return to France, if he would surrender all the secret and official documents in his possession. The negotiations were carried on for four months, as the Chevalier first demanded the payment of a certain sum of money which, he declared, was due to him, and eventually the Marquis returned to Paris. Another emissary was sent but without avail, and for a time the matter was dropped.

D'Eon was now getting impatient at the delay and at length got in touch with the famous Beaumarchais who undertook to reopen the negotiations. The Chevalier told him that he must have £5,333 in cash to pay Earl Ferrars, who had loaned him that amount on the documents which he held as security. He also handed him a massive key that he said opened the iron chest in which they were kept.

Beaumarchais set off for Paris with the key and, on arriving at Versailles, showed it to Broglie, who was so convinced that success in obtaining the documents was now assured that he empowered him to return to London with further overtures. Back in London in 1775, Beaumarchais received a letter from Vergennes stating that ' if M. d'Eon would disguise himself, everything would be settled.'

Whether it was due to this letter or the report that Louis XVI now really believed that he was a woman, the Chevalier no longer denied the statement that he was a female and in fact tacitly admitted it.

The iron chest containing the documents was said to be deposited at the town house of Earl Ferrars, in Upper Seymour Street, Portman Square, and Beaumarchais on learning this, obtained the Earl's authority to remove it on the payment of £4635 and bills for the balance. Without telling d'Eon, he removed it as quickly as possible and took it to Versailles, where, with great delight, he handed it over to Vergennes. The key was brought and the box was opened, when it was found, much to their chagrin, that the secret documents were missing and only some official papers of no great importance remained. Beaumarchais at once returned to London to inform d'Eon of the fact and he was greatly amused when he heard it.

" I knew that the secret correspondence and the most precious documents were not in the box," said the Chevalier smiling. " They are at my lodgings."

He then took Beaumarchais to Brewer Street and, removing a board in the floor of the bedroom, showed him a secret receptacle from which he took five cardboard letter-cases, sealed and labelled : ' Secret papers. To be given to the King only.' After another conference with d'Eon, Beaumarchais agreed to draw up a formal compact and on signing this the Chevalier finally made an inventory of the papers and then handed them over.

In this document d'Eon is formally described as a woman and in it agreed to assume the garments of the female sex on his return to France. He further agreed that ' he would declare that he was of that sex and would wear women's attire.'

Beaumarchais then left for Paris and returned shortly afterwards with two Royal warrants : one, a safe conduct for d'Eon's return to France, where he was to receive a yearly allowance of 12,000 livres ; and the other ordering his immediate resumption of ' the *garments of the female sex* which he was *never again to lay aside.*'

Beaumarchais also gave him the sum of 2000 crowns for the purchase of a suitable outfit, and it was agreed that all his male garments were to be left behind and sold in London. He then left for Paris, taking with him the precious papers, which he nearly lost overboard shortly after leaving Dover.

When the terms of d'Eon's agreement became known in London the craze for betting on his sex revived. Rumours of his departure caused a panic among those who had laid money on the question, one way or the other. It was stated that no less than £120,000 had been underwritten at various times, and the Chevalier was pressed and importuned to make a statement in order to settle all doubts. He then inserted a paragraph in the newspapers stating that he declined to reveal anything until all wagering ceased.

About this time Mr. Hayes, a surgeon, brought an action against a broker and underwriter to recover 700 guineas on which he had paid 15 guineas per cent premium. He agreed to return 100 guineas providing it was proved that d'Eon was actually a woman.

The trial resulted in a verdict for the plaintiff who produced as a witness a surgeon named Le Goux, who swore that ' to his certain knowledge, d'Eon was a woman as he had attended her in sickness and examined her person.'

The Chevalier made his first public appearance in London dressed as a woman on 6 August 1777, when it is said he wore ' an elegant sack with a head-dress adorned with diamonds.'

Shortly afterwards, he gave a farewell entertainment to some of his friends in Brewer Street, among whom were the two Angelos, the famous fencing-masters. One of them described d'Eon at that time as ' a lusty dame without the least beard, who was dressed in black silk with a head-dress in rosed toupet and a lace cap. She wore a diamond necklace, long stays, and an old-fashioned stomacher, and she saluted me with a kiss on each cheek.'

The Chevalier's creditor's, hearing of his early departure, now began to press d'Eon for debts he had contracted, so he authorized his landlady to sell his large and remarkable stock of wines for their ' benefit.' Meanwhile his clothes, weapons, furniture, and library of eight thousand books and two hundred manuscripts, were to remain in her charge, and for this he agreed to pay her twenty shillings a week rental.

He left for France on 13 August wearing his old red and green dragoon uniform and arrived in Paris. On presenting himself to Count de Vergennes he was told he must at once assume female attire as had been agreed, and he went off to stay at the house of M. Genest, whose two daughters, Madame Campan and Mademoiselle Adelaide Genest, were attached to the Royal household.

Madame Campan in her *Life and Times* says: ' D'Eon's deportment and behaviour were those of a grenadier. She dressed in black. Her hair is cut in a circle like a priest's and is plastered with pomade, powdered and surmounted by a black cap, such as pious ladies wear. She still wears flat round heels.'

Through these ladies the Queen, Marie Antoinette, heard of d'Eon's arrival in Paris, and she sent Genest an order to bring the Chevalier to see her. She showed such interest in him that she instructed her own milliner, Mademoiselle Bertin, ' to prepare the new woman an outfit such as would have sufficed for any four girls of the Royal House at St. Cyr,' and Sieur Brunet, the famous perruquier of the rue de la Paroisse, received an order for a head-dress composed of three tiers.'

The Chevalier, disconcerted at these efforts to transform him into a woman, says: ' Mlle Bertin undertakes to turn me into a passably modest and obedient woman. Only my extreme desire to appear irreproachable in the eyes of the King and my protectors, could impart to me the strength I need to conquer myself and adopt a mildness of disposition in conformity with the new existence which has been forced upon me. It would be easier for me to play the part of a lion than that of a lamb.'

However, d'Eon became the rage and excited the greatest interest wherever he went. People from the provinces flocked to Paris, anxious to obtain a glimpse of this remarkable person of ' unknown ' sex about whom there was so much mystery. His portraits were in the shop windows and his name on everyone's lips. Voltaire went to see him, and afterwards remarked that ' the Chevalier's case was a nice problem for history.'

At length, the notoriety thrust upon him became unbearable and d'Eon sought every possible means of getting rid of his feminine attire. In 1779, he applied to the authorities for permission to serve as a naval volunteer in the Fleet at Brest, but this was met with a direct refusal.

Later, in sheer desperation, he abandoned his petticoats and put on his old dragoon uniform once more. This change of costume was soon noticed and reported to the authorities ; he was arrested and sent to Dijon, where he was kept a prisoner for three months.

When he returned to Paris in September of that year, he once more assumed female attire, but the publicity made his life so unbearable that he sought refuge at Tonnerre, the place of his birth, and lived there quietly for some years.

At the conclusion of the war in September 1783, he applied for permission to go to London to settle his affairs. When this was granted, he once more set out for England and eventually settled in his old lodgings in Brewer Street, accompanied by a maid. He continued to dress as a woman for fear of losing his annuity, on which, it was said, he was now entirely dependent. In order to get money he decided to turn his skill in fencing to account and gave both public and private performances. Clad as Joan of Arc in full armour and wearing a casque with a plume, he appeared before the Prince of Wales at the King's Theatre.

In 1788, he sold all his books and manuscripts at Christie's, and a subscription was raised to help him to which the Prince of Wales gave £100. The sale of his jewellery and snuff-boxes followed, which realized £348 17s. 7d., and with the proceeds of the sales he paid off his creditors and then applied for permission to return to France to join the Army.

Meanwhile the situation in France had become so disturbed and uncertain it was impolitic for him to go back. His annuity had ceased, and in 1792 he again endeavoured to raise money by giving exhibition displays of fencing. He gave one at Carlton House in the presence of the Prince of Wales, and others at Devonshire House, the Club d'Armes in Brewer Street and at the Haymarket Theatre. They were so successful and drew such large crowds, that a provincial tour was arranged and he appeared at Brighton, Bath, and Oxford.

On 26 August 1796, while giving a display at Southampton, he received from his opponent a thrust in the right armpit which completely disabled him. The wound proved serious and on his return to London he was obliged to remain in bed for a considerable time. He took apartments with a Mrs. Cole, a French-woman by birth, who as he became weaker nursed and looked after him. Now, too, age began to tell on him, and as he was too feeble to give further fencing lessons he was reduced to poverty. His old friends did what they could to help him, and the Duke of Queensbury is said to have allowed him fifty pounds a year.

In 1808, when he was in his eightieth year, almost bedridden and quite incapable, Mrs. Cole, who remained by him through his illness, removed to 26 New Milman Street, Bloomsbury, near the Found-ling Hospital, and there he died on 21 May 1810, at the age of eighty-one.

On examination of the body after his death, an autopsy was ordered, which was carried out by a surgeon, Mr. Thomas Copeland, in the presence of the Earl of Yarborough and Sir Sydney Smith. The surgeon certified that ' d'Eon de Beaumont was of *the masculine sex* and *of that sex only*,' and so dispelled all the doubts and speculations which had so long surrounded him during his strange career. He had kept the secret and mystery of his sex to the last, for even Mrs. Cole, who befriended him and with whom he lived his later years, is said to have firmly believed that her companion was a woman and was astounded when she heard the result of the surgeon's examination. He was buried in the graveyard of St. Pancras Church on 28 May 1810.

Thus ended d'Eon de Beaumont, whose extraordinary career for more than half a century attracted interest and attention throughout Europe. He was well-called a ' Prince ' of impersonators. As a diplomatist he was a shrewd but impetuous intriguer. As a soldier his courage was never questioned. He was constantly embroiled in political troubles which were not always of his own making and so became a victim of the strange circumstances which surrounded his life.

IN the early part of 1830 a young and beautiful Irish girl was living in apartments in Union Court, Orchard Street, Westminster. She had a wealth of light brown hair which she wore curled in ringlets in the fashion of the time, and they formed a perfect setting to her lovely face, while her figure was graceful and slim, and her whole appearance gentle and refined.

She gave out that she was an actress and her name Lavinia Edwards, although sometimes she was known on the stage as ' Miss Walstein.' She had never performed in London, although she frequently appeared in the provinces, and had played at the Norwich Theatre and latterly at Tewkesbury, taking leading parts in tragedies.

She was later joined in her rooms in Union Court by another Irish girl of about seventeen whom she introduced as her sister. The name of this girl was Maria Edwards, and she was said to have come from Dublin. The couple lived quietly together, their only visitors being the men who called on them at various times. They appeared to have no regular source of income, nor did they seek engagements, although they lived close to the Coburg Theatre. It transpired later on that Lavinia was living under the protection of a Mr. Thomas Smith, who supplied the girls with means and looked after them.

In January 1833, Lavinia was taken ill and on the request of Mr. Smith a Dr. Somerville was called in to attend her and he found her suffering from a severe inflammation of the lungs. About three o'clock on the morning of the 23rd, she roused Maria, who was sleeping with her, and complained of a ' wheezing in the throat,' and it was evident that she was in a serious condition.

" Maria, I am dying," she murmured. " It has pleased God to call me."

In about five minutes she was dead.

An inquest was held at Westminster on 25 January 1833 by order of the Home Secretary, and as there were no claimants to the body it was taken to Guy's Hospital for examination. Here it was discovered that the body was that of a man of very feminine appearance. He had no sign of a beard beyond that of a boy of seventeen, and the whiskers on the face had evidently been removed with tweezers. The hair was light brown and about two feet long, of a soft glossy texture, and the whole appearance of the face was that of a woman.

At the inquest Dr. Clutterbuck stated that he had examined the body at the request of Dr. Somerville, who had attended the supposed girl a few weeks before ; he used the name of ' Lavinia Edwards ' at his lodgings near the Coburg Theatre and was suffering from a dangerous inflammation of the lungs. The doctor had no idea that ' Lavinia Edwards ' was not a woman as he had attended her previously at the request of Mr. Smith, under whose protection he understood she had been living. She had a very feminine appearance and a kind of cracked voice not unlike a female.

Maria Edwards was then called and said she passed as Lavinia's sister. She was seventeen years of age, while Lavinia was twenty-four and was born in Dublin. They had lived together constantly for about ten years. She earned her living by performing on the stage, travelling about the country and playing female characters. In the provinces she played under the name of ' Miss Edwards ' in the first line of tragedy, but she had also used the name of ' Walstein.' They had been living in London about three years and were supported by different gentlemen.

Mary Mortimer, living at Union Court, stated that she had known the deceased for ten or eleven years, but had never known her real sex until that day. She had every reason to believe that she had died a natural death. She always appeared as a most lady-like woman and had played at the Norwich Theatre. She had slept with her repeatedly and had no idea she was a man.

Mrs. Shellett stated that she collected the rents in Union Court. The deceased and her sister were not very regular in paying. She had heard her coughing and thought at the time it was a man.

Mr. Alfred Taylor, a surgeon of Guy's Hospital, deposed that he examined the body and made a post-mortem on it. He found the stomach perfectly healthy but the liver much diseased. It presented the appearance seen in persons addicted to drink which is commonly called a ' drunkard's liver.' He discovered that the deceased was a perfect man.

Mr. Ollier, another surgeon, corroborated the last witness and at this stage a man came forward and asked if he could give evidence. On being given permission, he said he had seen it stated in the papers that the deceased had come from Dublin and he was now satisfied that he knew the party. About twelve or thirteen years ago the deceased sometimes passed as a *woman* and sometimes as a *man*. He had lately performed on the stage in the country in some principal tragic characters. He never knew the deceased had a sister.

On viewing the body the jury were completely astounded and one member remarked : " It is almost impossible." Another exclaimed : " Look at the head of hair and the ears pierced for ear-rings ! "

while a third declared : " It is the most extraordinary case I ever met with. I almost doubt the evidence of my own senses."

In the end, the jury stated that they were completely satisfied as to the identity of the body and returned a verdict ' That the deceased died by the visitation of God and the jury are compelled to express their horror at the unnatural conduct of the deceased, and strongly recommend the proper authorities that some means may be adopted in the disposal of the body which will mark the ignominy of the crime.'

It is evident from the account of the inquiry that the case of ' Lavinia Edwards ' was one of inversion, but the natural appearance of effeminacy greatly enabled him to conceal his sex with success. This, together with the fact that he was accustomed to appear on the stage in male as well as female parts, had doubtless helped him to deceive even those who had known him intimately for so long a period.

WHO was the person known as Jenny de Savalette de Lange who for fifty years was believed to be a woman and who died at Versailles on 6 May 1858 ? His sex was never once detected or even suspected during the long period of his strange career.

Whether he posed as a female for his own reasons or was forced to adopt women's attire it is impossible to say ; judging however from the stories of his life it is probable that circumstances rather than inclination induced him to conceal his true sex, for he was always endeavouring to extract money from people of high station in life and even tried to get a ' husband ' to keep him.

In 1816, as ' Jenny,' he became engaged to M. Albert de T——, of the King's Bodyguard, who was succeeded as fiancé by Monsieur M. N., a Captain in a cavalry regiment. Another lover was M. Delpy de Lacipière, an officer serving in the Paris Garrison, who for fifteen years remained a suitor. Even when he was ordered to Corsica ' she ' kept on imploring him to marry her. Their correspondence was kept up until 1831, although he knew marriage was impossible, and then a quarrel took place on financial matters.

Although he appears to have attracted some half a dozen suitors, from the description we have of him, even when made up as a woman he could hardly be said to have had any personal charm. No portrait of ' Jenny ' is said to exist, but a description, probably biased, has been left by one of ' her ' discarded lovers.

He says she was 'tall, thin, and lop-sided, and she leaned on an umbrella. Her features were hard ; her look stern and her voice shrill and cracked. She wore a dress that dated from the Empire or the Restoration, and on her head a black cap surmounted by a broad-brimmed hat. She took snuff frequently and had such a masculine appearance that people who passed in the street used to say : " How much she resembles a man."'

There are several stories relating to the strange career of this person, none of which however can be vouched for as being absolutely true, as they vary much in detail and disagree in dates.

On 7 November 1820, a statement on oath was sworn before a *juge de paix* that Savalette de Lange was the illegitimate daughter of Charles Pierre Paul Savalette de Lange, but that she did not know the name of her mother nor where she was born, and was unable to produce a certificate of birth.

Many French writers refer to her, and among others Gabrielle Anne de Cisterne de Courtiras in her *Memoires des Autres*. She states : 'Mademoiselle de —— was an only daughter and inherited all the papers belonging to her father, which contained proofs of his great services to the House of Bourbon. There are five or six versions of her history, but the one I am going to narrate seems to be supported by probabilities which are almost proofs.

' The man who possessed all the papers had been the confidential servant of M. de ——. He knew the family and their connections and that after the death of the father and daughter, the family would become extinct. He accompanied them when they emigrated. When Comte de —— died he remained along with the daughter, gained her confidence and murdered her for the sake of the documents. These, however, would be useless to him if he could not pass himself off as Mademoiselle de —— herself.

' He went to another town and dressed as a woman. This he could easily do as he was young and of small stature, while what little beard he had was blonde. Having made the metamorphosis he sought to turn it into profit. He wrote to everybody he could think of asking their assistance and dwelling on the services his father had rendered and so obtained as much money as he needed.'

At the time of the alleged emigration the real Mademoiselle de Lange was six or seven years old and doubt is thrown on this story owing to another statement, in which it is declared that the Comte de Lange did not emigrate.

If the real ' Jenny ' did disappear and an impostor took her place, it must have occurred between 1804 and 1812, for according to evidence brought forward by Alfred Begis, ' Jenny ' was present at a ball given by the Austrian ambassador in honour of Marie Louise on 18 July 1810.

By other writers it is suggested that ' Jenny ' was the missing Louis XVII who made his escape from the Temple, but this is pure conjecture and cannot be entertained as credible.

Next we come to the narrative related by M. G. Lenôtre in 1900. He tells us that ' Charles Pierre Paul Savalette de Lange started off for Brittany with his daughter Jenny during the period of the Revolution. At Orleans they made the acquaintance of an elegant and plausible young gentleman who made out that he knew Brittany well and offered his services as guide to the Comte and his daughter. They went to St. Malo together and there met a young lady who was accompanied by an old servant called Robin, to whose care she had been committed with orders to bring her safely to Plymouth where her parents awaited her. The young man agreed to take charge of the party and arranged with the captain of a foreign vessel to take them to Plymouth. But they never reached there, for no sooner were they out to sea than the captain informed them he was bound for Hamburg and had no intention of calling at Plymouth.' Everyone agreed to this with the exception of old Robin, who was so grieved that he was unable to fulfil his promise to the parents of the young lady he had in his care, that he took ill and died after an attack of fever three days after they arrived in Hamburg. It therefore devolved on the young man to let the father and mother of Mademoiselle know where their daughter was and he is supposed to have written to them but received no reply. Some months passed, and by that time the little party had come to an end of their resources.

Later on the Comte de Savalette de Lange died of 'putrid fever' and his daughter Jenny, now without means, wrote to the Comte d'Artois to remind him of some money her father had lent him, but her appeal was without avail, and, worn out by disappointment and probably starvation, she too fell ill and died.

In this way the young man came into possession of all her papers and began to write begging letters in her name, but without success. The other girl in the party, who is alluded to as Mademoiselle C——, eventually became the mistress of the young man, designated B, and they lived together until the Revolution was over and they were able to return to France. The parents or relatives of Mademoiselle C—— took her home and the young man disappeared.

Mademoiselle C—— afterwards lived a quiet retired life until 1810, when she met the Comte de R——, who fell in love with her. He married her and they went to live in the Rue de las P—— in the Marais quarter.

One day in 1815 a tall, gaunt woman with her hair done in plain bands and her face closely veiled, presented herself at the Comte's apartments. Her appearance was unassuming, although she wore a gaudily trimmed bonnet with large strings. She asked for Madame de R—— and when she was alone with her, raised her veil and disclosed the face of the man B——.

" I am your old friend, Jenny Savalette de Lange," he said. He then explained to his former mistress that he wanted to use that name to extract money from the Royal family, but in order to do that, he needed the help of Madame de R—— to testify his identity.

Madame de R—— bowed her head and fearing disgrace and dishonour to the name she then bore, consented to help him.

He was thus enabled to play the part, until Madame de R——, stricken by the thought of aiding such an imposture, revealed the truth to her husband.

On finding this out, B—— took fright and hid himself at Versailles until his death, when his real sex was discovered.

Such is the story given by M. Lenôtre, who states the true name of Mademoiselle C—— was Mademoiselle de Tinteniac, who married the Comte de Saint Roman in 1810.

The next heard of ' Jenny ' is a reference to her seeking a situation as governess with a family. She declared she was a protégée of Madame de Bourbonne and later, when she appears to have retired to Paris, she went to live at a Maison des Bains in the rue Taranne, where she is supposed to have been in receipt of a pension from the Emperor granted in July 1812.

At the fall of the Empire the pension ceased, but as soon as the King was established and restored to the throne, she renewed her petitions vigorously and again pressed her claim for all the great services that had been rendered to the Royal family by M. de

Savalette. In 1814, she again demanded the payment of the loan made by her father to Comte d'Artois, and later it is stated she received pensions from Louis XVIII and Charles IX.

There are records in support of the statement that in May 1822, Jenny Savalette de Lange was made postmistress of Poligny, but she apparently never took the post, for later on she was given a similar position at Villejuif near Paris, with a salary of 1200 francs.

In the same year she endeavoured to obtain an apartment in the Château Versailles and eventually succeeded, for her address was given as 'Marble Court, Staircase 13. Second floor. Door 66.' There she is said to have lived until 1832. On the death of Louis XVIII in 1824 she lost her pension but, as stated, it was restored and increased by Charles IX in 1825, while she is said to have also had an allowance from the Duchesse d'Angoulême.

The upheaval in France in 1830 reduced her to penury and she again renewed her appeals to various royal personages, among others to Queen Marie Amélie, pressing her claims on the Bourbon family and asking if she could have a post as vendor of stamped paper.

Later, when the Château Versailles was turned into a museum she had to give up her apartment and return to Paris, but only for a time, for she went back to Versailles and took an apartment in the rue du Marché Neuf. There she lived for five years and died after a short illness in 1858.

When two women were called in to render the necessary offices to the dead, they discovered to their amazement the body was that of a man. They at once informed the civil authorities of this fact and Dr. Dugué was instructed to make an inspection and report. He certified that 'it was not permitted to doubt that the late Mademoiselle Jenny Savalette de Lange was of the masculine sex.'

The official document made on Thursday, 6 May 1858, at the hour of noon, reads : ' Certificate of death of unknown man having borne the name of Henriette Jenny Savalette de Lange, bachelor, of no profession, born at (place cannot be stated) in the year 1790. Died this day 2 a.m. at his residence 11 Rue du Marché Neuf, Versailles.' Then follow the names of the Registrar, witnesses, and the Mayor of Versailles.

Among the articles found in the apartment was a magnificent bed-cover of fine guipure lace which had belonged to the Royal family, with coats of arms, armorial bearings, dolphins, and other emblems worked in the design. When it came to be sold, it was discovered that it had originally been the bed-cover used by Louis XIV, and it was purchased by the State. How it came into the possession of ' Jenny ' remained a mystery.

The real identity of this person who posed and lived as a woman for over half a century has never been established. That he had intimate friends among women there seems little doubt, but they never seem to have suspected the deception which he carried on to the day of his death.

Having by some means obtained knowledge of the affairs of Savalette de Lange he turned it to account with adroit cunning and so imposed on the highest personages in France that he was successful in obtaining pensions which kept him for the greater part of his life.

He was never known to have worn men's clothes or to have betrayed his true sex, so it is probable that he was brought up and educated as a girl, but nothing is known of his early life. Many of the stories concerning him cannot be authenticated and so the identity of the man who posed as Jenny de Savalette de Lange remains a mystery still.

A CURIOUS case of female impersonation by a notorious gangster was brought to light in America during a trial that took place in Chicago in 1923.

The accused, who was known as the 'Smiling Bandit Queen,' was acquitted of the charge of murder, but his career, which was related in court, excited great interest at the time.

One night in June 1923, when a Mr. and Mrs. Tasmer were putting their car into the garage, they were attacked by two people. The one, who fired a shot that hit Mr. Tasmer, was apparently a woman, and as the pistol was discharged Mrs. Tasmer saw the assailant's face, which she declared she would never forget. The police arrested many female suspects, but eventually thinking that the bandit might have been a man masquerading as a woman, watched an apartment which was occupied by a chauffeur who lived there with a person known as 'his wife.' Early one morning the wife was hurriedly arrested and, while still in her night-clothes and a kimono, was brought before Mrs. Tasmer, the wife of the murdered man, who at once positively identified 'her' by her smile.

During the following day, the supposed wife acquired such a stubbly beard beneath her powder and rouge that her sex was no longer in doubt.

The police discovered 'she' was no other than a well-known gangster, and on being questioned he revealed his real name.

'God gave me a double nature,' he told the police, when he related some account of his life. He declared that he had been born in Columbus, Ohio, and as a child was naturally quiet and although brought up as a boy, he always wanted to wear girl's clothes. At the age of fourteen he was turned out of his home by his father and in 1912 had married a man at Crown Point, Indiana. He came to Chicago at the age of fifteen and was now thirty-two. When still a youth, he had adopted girl's clothes and first took a situation as a chambermaid. Later, having a high soprano voice, he became singer in a cabaret. He and the ' husband ' were arrested in 1912 and ordered to produce their marriage licence which they did. Twelve years afterwards he married a girl, which so enraged the ' husband ' that a fight ensued, but it ended in all three living together in a strange compact.

At the trial the accused appeared in court in silk garments, though wearing trousers, while his hair was braided over his ears. The trousers were of satin, his shirt waistcoat open, and his face rouged. He spoke in the low tones a woman would have used, nervously clasped and unclasped his hands and sobbed when he told of his double life.

When asked if he shot Mr. Tasmer, he replied : " No, gentlemen. I could not kill a cat or a dog." Then, uncovering his face with his hands, he wept hysterically.

The judge after questioning him, involuntarily remarked : " That will be all, *lady*."

When questioned as to where he was on the night of the murder, he replied : " I was at home that evening."

Mrs. Tasmer, however, positively identified him as the ' laughing blue-eyed girl ' who had shot her husband, but it was shown that the eyes of the accused were *grey*.

The jury after deliberating for two hours returned

with a verdict of ' Not guilty,' and the prisoner was acquitted.

After his release he again assumed feminine dress and was engaged to appear in a Chicago vaudeville theatre, but the police intervened and stopped the performance.

He applied for an injunction against the authorities, and again appeared in court attired in a fashionable up-to-date sports costume and wearing a closely fitting toque. He was unsuccessful in his application, and it was remarked in court that in women's clothing he seemed a woman and not by any means a masculine one.

Another eccentric person who is said to have habitually worn female dress was thus described in the *Milwaukee Journal*. ' He lived on an island on Lake Superior between Canada and the United States and kept aloof from everyone. He wore women's clothes, shoes, ear-rings and a corset by day, and went to bed in a lacy night-gown.' This curious impersonation is said to have been due to a love-affair in youth which ended tragically in the death of the man's sweetheart. In memory of her he dressed in the lace clothes and the high-heeled shoes she affected. The shoes, with high French heels, he made himself and walked in them as daintily as a girl. If he wore those of a tan colour he used white laces, or if white tops he laced them with black. The style he favoured had tan uppers with black patent leather below with pointed toes and white laces. ' At the foot of his bed,' says the narrator, ' was a pile of women's shoes, numbering at least fifty and each pair had been made by himself. Some days he wore overalls, but usually a pair of shorts which came below the knees. He earned a living by building boats and was rarely seen without a corn-cob pipe in his mouth.'

XXVII

THE mystery surrounding the death of a clever young government official in 1926 who called himself ' Madame Cartier,' has never been satisfactorily solved. His real name was R—— de la C—— and he held a post in the Ministry of Agriculture in Paris, where he was regarded as an able and brilliant Civil Servant. He was a married man with two daughters, but for some months he had been living alone in the furnished apartment where he was found dead. He had not been seen for some little time, and suspicions were aroused one morning in 1926. His apartment was opened by the police, who found his body hanging from a hook in the ceiling of his drawing-room. His hands and feet were securely bound and a scarf had been used as a noose. He had been dead for some time when discovered, and it was noticed that as the body hung from the stout hook from which it was suspended it was reflected in a full-length mirror standing against the wall of the room.

It was concluded that he had committed suicide, but why, before doing so, he should have dressed himself in woman's clothes was the question which puzzled the authorities. To their amazement, when the body was examined, he was found to be attired as a fashionable woman in every detail, including stockings of fine silk, many-coloured garters, and lace lingerie.

As far as was known he had lived the normal life of a clever respected official, and he was known to his friends as an affable and even-tempered man. What reason could he have, they asked, for wearing feminine costume ?

Some light was afterwards thrown on the mystery when it was learnt that a *modiste* had been accustomed to sending parcels of lingerie to a ' Madame Cartier ' at M. de la C——'s address. When the police began to trace ' Madame Cartier,' in order to find out if she knew of the death of M. de la C——, they found she was well known in the night-life of Montmartre, but had disappeared and had not been seen for some time. Comparing the descriptions they obtained of the lady with photographs they found in the apartment, the police eventually concluded that M. de la C—— and ' Madame Cartier ' were one and the same person. Carrying their inquiries further they discovered that ' Madame ' had been regarded as queen of the night-life in Montmartre for some time, and in the cafés and studios she frequented was well known for her wit and undeniable good looks.

She preferred the company of men at dinners and as partners in dancing, and beyond a few girl friends she was rarely seen with women. Though popular with men, when ' Madame ' left her haunts at Montmartre, usually after midnight, she always forbade anyone to follow her.

One girl who knew her well told the police that while she did not know her friend was a man, she frequently suspected it and knew that ' Cartier ' was not her real name. Others said they knew ' Madame ' had assumed the name, but they had no idea she was a man.

After all inquiries had been concluded, no reason other than mental derangement could be assigned for suicide, but there seems little doubt that homosexuality was the real reason for his masquerading as a woman in the night haunts of Paris.

PART THREE

Claimants to Royal and Other Titles

XXVIII

WHETHER the person known as Perkin Warbeck, who claimed to be Richard, Duke of York and son of Edward IV, was an impostor or not, was a question which greatly excited this country towards the close of the fifteenth century. The story of this mysterious young man is now an almost forgotten page in English history.

According to his reputed confession printed shortly before his execution, he was born at Tournai about 1474, and was the son of John Osbeck, controller of that city, by his wife Catherine de Faro. The name Osbeck is apparently a variation of Warbeck, for his father, according to the archives of Tournai, is called Jehan de Werbecque, and was a Jew.

According to one story the father had been to London in the reign of Edward IV, and during that time his wife Catherine had been delivered of a son. Being in favour at Court, Werbecque persuaded the King to stand godfather to the child, though it was hinted by some that there was in reality a much nearer connexion between the King and the boy. This, it was thought, accounted for the resemblance afterwards remarked between young Perkin and the Monarch.

When still a youth, it is said that Perkin's mother took him to Antwerp to stay with a cousin, but owing to the wars in Flanders he returned to Tournai about 1483. A year later, a merchant named Berlo took him again to Antwerp, his native city, where he was taken ill, but afterwards found service at Middelburg.

Some months later he went to Portugal in company with the wife of Sir Edward Brampton, an adherent of the House of York, and after remaining with her a year he took service with a knight named Peter Vacz de Cogna.

The next heard of him was when he landed in Cork in 1491, ' richly dressed in fine silk which was said to have belonged to his master.'

He assumed the name of Richard, Duke of York, son of Edward IV, and soon many rallied to his side.

Only four years previously Lambert Simnel, another impersonator, had been crowned in Dublin as the son of the Duke of Clarence, and many people declared that Perkin was the same son of Clarence who had been so crowned. He, however, denied this story, but finding that the Earls of Desmond and Kildare were ready to support him, he agreed to take on the character of the Duke of York.

He was taught English and instructed how to deport himself as became the son of a royal house.

On 2 March 1492, James IV of Scotland received a letter from him in which he called himself ' King Edward's son.'

The news that the ' Duke of York ' had arrived in Ireland soon reached France, and Charles VIII, then on the point of war with King Henry of England, invited him to come to Paris.

On his arrival he was received with all the marks of respect due to the rightful heir to the British throne.

Perkin's deportment, it is said, now left nothing to be desired, and his personal qualities supported the opinion which was spread abroad of his Royal ancestry. His story began to gain credence in England, and Sir George Neville, Sir George Taylor, and over a hundred other gentlemen went to Paris to offer their services to the pseudo-Duke of York and to share his fortunes.

Henry VII, now alarmed at Perkin's success in France in gaining such a powerful friend as Charles, hurriedly concluded a treaty of peace with France and

PERKIN WARBECK
(From an early drawing.)

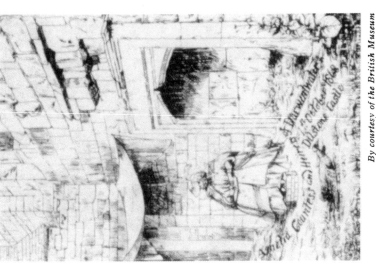

AMELIA 'COUNTESS OF
DERWENTWATER'

(From a drawing by herself when
she occupied the ruins of Dilstone
Castle, October 1st, 1868.)

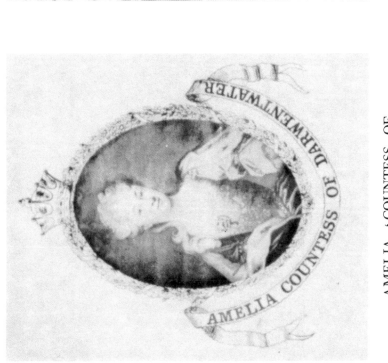

AMELIA 'COUNTESS OF
DERWENTWATER'

Perkin went off to Flanders to seek the protection of Margaret, Dowager-Duchess of Burgundy, who is said to have always believed that her nephew, Richard Plantagenet, Duke of York, had escaped from the Tower. She gave him a cordial reception, acknowledged him as her nephew, and designated him as the ' White Rose of England.' Her recognition caused many others in England to embrace Perkin's cause. On Henry VII protesting against support being given to the pretender in Flanders, Perkin departed in November 1493, and next presented himself to Maximilian, King of the Romans, at Vienna.

In the summer of 1494 Maximilian brought him to the Low Countries once more, and gave him recognition as King of England. Garter King-of-Arms was at once sent from London to remonstrate against this action and declared to both Maximilian and the Duchess of Burgundy that King Henry had positive evidence of Perkin being the son of a citizen of Tournai. In October we find that Perkin was present at Antwerp when the Archduke Philip took his oath as Duke of Brabant and he displayed the arms of the House of York outside the place where he stayed.

Meanwhile Henry showed great ingenuity in detecting the origin of this mysterious person who so boldly made pretensions to his throne. Plotting was found to be going on in England in his favour, so Henry sent spies to Flanders who insinuated themselves among Perkin's friends. They bribed his retainers and servants and even his confessor, and brought back a full account of the conspiracy and those who were fomenting it. The King next offered pardon to Sir Robert Clifford and William Barley, two of Perkin's strongest supporters. Clifford accepted the pardon and on returning to England received a reward of five hundred pounds for supplying information. A number of Perkin's adherents were then suddenly arrested in Flanders, and the Duchess Margaret of Burgundy, who had been so long at enmity with King Henry, received a deed from her supposed nephew in which he engaged to restore to her the revenues granted to her by Edward IV on her marriage, which had long been a bone of contention.

Perkin, by means of loans, had managed to get a little fleet together of which he took command. His ships appeared off Deal on 3 July and landed a small body of men, but the Kentish folk and fishermen fell on the invaders, killed 150 of them and took 80 prisoners. He next sailed for Ireland and laid seige to Waterford, but without success. He then turned his attention to Scotland, where he was more fortunate, for James IV received him at Stirling and called him ' the true prince.' He further gave him in marriage Lady Catherine Gordon, a daughter of the Earl of Huntly, his own cousin, and planned an invasion of England. Perkin as ' Duke of York ' also wrote to the Earl of Desmond to send forces to his aid from Ireland, and issued a proclamation in England as King, but few answered to the call although the Scots began to raid the border. James, however, at last grew tired of the contest and consented to treat with Henry.

Perkin remained in Scotland until July 1497, and then, fearing he might be given up, embarked with his wife and child in a Breton merchant ship aided by two expert seamen, Andrew and Robert Barton, who accompanied him in their own vessels.

He first made another attempt to land in Ireland, but finding no support either from Kildare or Desmond, he crossed the sea and finally made for Cornwall, which county had recently rallied to his cause.

He landed at Whitesand Bay and at once proclaimed himself ' Richard IV.' Recruits came to his standard and he found himself at the head of a small army of over three thousand men.

He first marched on Exeter, but was driven off by the citizens, and learning of the approach of a large army under the Earl of Devonshire he withdrew to Taunton. Here again he was checked, and on hearing that Lord Daubeny was marching against him he stole away at midnight with sixty horsemen, whom he abandoned, and with only three he rode on to Beaulieu in Hampshire, where he sought sanctuary.

Two companies of the King's horse presently surrounded the place and Perkin, realizing the game was up, surrendered to the King's mercy. He was taken to Taunton where Henry arrived on 5 October and, having been promised his life, he made a full confession. King Henry then went to Exeter and dispatched a troop of horse to St. Michael's Mount, where Perkin had left his wife and child, with instructions to bring them to him.

After seeing Lady Catherine, the King made Perkin confess his imposture once more, and then sent his wife under escort to the Queen, ' assuring her of his desire that she should be treated as a sister.'

The country now being quiet, King Henry returned to London taking Perkin with him. He was paraded through the streets as an object of derision and then lodged in the Tower.

He was released soon afterwards and kept in the King's Court without restraint, but a careful watch was kept on him.

On 9 June 1498 he made an attempt to escape and managed to reach the monastery of Syon, where he surrendered once more on pardon. As punishment, on Friday, 15 June, he was placed in the stocks, which were raised on scaffolding reared on barrels at Westminster Hall and afterwards in Cheapside, where he remained for five hours during which he repeated his confession. Afterwards he was once more lodged in the Tower.

In 1499 he made an attempt to bribe his keeper, who on a pretence of yielding brought him into communication with other prisoners including the Earl of Warwick. A plot was formed to seize the Tower which being discovered, Perkin and his friend John à Water, Mayor of Cork, and two others, were condemned to death at Westminster.

On Saturday, 23 November 1499, Perkin Warbeck and John à Water were hanged at Tyburn after confessing their misdeeds.

After his execution his widow resumed her maiden name of Gordon and received a pension from the King, who treated her very liberally. Later she married James Strangeways, a gentleman-usher of the King's chamber.

On the death of her second husband she married Matthias Cradock and obtained permission to live in Wales. When Cradock died she married for the fourth time one Christopher Ashton, with whom she lived at Fyfield in Berkshire, where she died in 1537.

XXIX

IMPERSONATION of Royal personages has occurred in history from time to time and the impostor has generally been discovered, but the identity of the remarkable woman who called herself ' Duchess of Aybelen ' and impersonated Anne of Cleves remains a mystery to this day.

The story begins in the winter of the year 1558 when John Frederick II, Elector of Saxony, on his return home from a journey at Eisenach found two letters awaiting him. They were written in a somewhat illegible feminine hand, dated from Eckartsberg and signed, ' Anne, Duchess of Aybelen, widow of Duke Henry of Shyprus in Ireland.'

The writer begged the Elector to send some trustworthy person to her as she had important matters to communicate respecting Queen Anne of England, the wife of King Henry VIII.

Queen Anne, or Anne of Cleves as she was generally called, was the aunt of the Elector John Frederick and his mother's sister. He had strongly objected to her marriage at the time, but his objections were unheeded and on 31 December 1539, Anne of Cleves landed at Dover and the next day travelled to Rochester where King Henry, her future husband, awaited her.

She was a big, strongly-built girl, ungainly in her movements and by no means beautiful. It is therefore not to be wondered that the fickle Henry was disillusioned directly he saw her and could scarcely conceal his disappointment at her appearance. It is said that he could hardly make up his mind to give her the presents he had brought for her, and after the official reception he bitterly reproached those who he declared had brought him ' a great Flanders mare.'

Unable to find any valid excuse for breaking his engagement with the Princess at the last moment, Henry married her on 6 January 1540.

Scarcely six months had elasped when pretty Catherine Howard captured the changeable monarch's heart, and Anne, after being sent off to Richmond, was informed that the King intended to divorce her. She consented to abide by the decision of the Church, and soon afterwards the marriage was declared null and void. Queen Anne was allotted Richmond Palace as a residence together with an annuity of £3000 a year and rank immediately after the Queen and the Royal children. The divorced Queen passed the remainder of her days at Richmond (or Chelsea) until she died on 16 July 1557.

It was about eighteen months after her death, which had been duly announced to her family and the Courts of Europe, that her nephew, the Elector, received the letters from the ' Duchess Anne.' John Frederick replied to them, and after some correspondence eventually sent one of his squires to the lady with a letter of introduction. The mysterious ' Duchess of Aybelen,' however, refused to make him the confidant of her secrets and demanded an interview with the Elector himself.

John Frederick then sent his secretary, John Rudolf, to the lady with a personal letter signed by himself, in which he told her she might place implicit confidence in its bearer.

The ' Duchess ' then unburdened her mind to the trusty Rudolf and told him the following extraordinary story. She said that she had succeeded in escaping from a London prison by means of a knotted rope and had found shelter on board a ship which brought her to Danzig. There she met with Queen Anne of England who had also managed to escape from the place in which she had been detained.

After passing through many adventures during twelve months, the ' Duchess ' had lost all her money, but the reason she was so anxious to speak to the Elector, was to tell him that his aunt—*Anne of Cleves, Queen of England—was still alive* and that her treasures had been secured and brought to Germany. A merchant whose life she had at one time saved had undertaken to convey these treasures to Augsburg and hand them to one Jobst Reffhausen, who had large dealings with England on account of the Fuggers, the famous bankers.

Among the treasures she enumerated were the ' Sceptre, Imperial globe and Crown of England, the English privileges (?), and a necklace of diamonds with a carbuncle,' for all of which she held regular receipts.

There were also deposited with the same merchant, and equally belonging to the Queen, ' 24 barrels of gold in crowns with the Imperial effigy, seven dresses all embroidered with fine pearls, three others of cloth of gold, 14 gold chains weighing 5000 crowns, 24 bracelets of the weight of 2000 crowns, 14 girdles and waistbelts weighing 7000 crowns, 12 head-dresses of fine pearls, and 14 necklaces weighing 3000 crowns.'

The Queen had sent William von Zieritz to fetch all this treasure and was obliged to await his return ; but if the Elector would send her a trustworthy man she would give him and his brothers the 24 barrels of gold, while the Sceptre, the Globe, and ' the privileges ' she reserved for another occasion. She further said that ' the Queen also intended to write to the King of France to induce him to give his daughter in marriage to John Frederick and then she would make him another present from the treasures and " privileges " of the noble crown of England.' As a measure of prudence, the Queen had not communicated with the Elector direct, but would do so if all went as she wished.

The ' Duchess ' showed the secretary her signet as a pledge, calling his attention to the fact that it was of solid gold. Finally, she implored him to arrange matters so that her departure for Augsburg might take place before the opening of the Diet of Empire, so that no part of the rich windfall might slip from the Elector. In the meanwhile she was proceeding to Russia, and she asked to be supplied with a good stock of game and Rhenish wine.

It is amazing that this incredible and extraordinary story should have been believed even at the close of the sixteenth century, when news travelled so slowly. One would have thought that its utter improbability alone would have created doubt in the mind of the Elector, but apparently he swallowed it all.

He wrote to the ' Duchess ' and thanked her for the information and gave orders that she was to be supplied with the ' game and wine together with fabrics to make her suitable dresses.'

He further made up his mind to see the lady herself and an interview was arranged. At this meeting she made the astonishing declaration that *she* was none other than Anne of Cleves, his own aunt. The Elector immediately accepted her statement, for he at once wrote to his brother, John William, who was then in Paris, acquainting him of the interview and saying that he found ' an astonishing likeness between the features of the lady and a portrait of Anne of Cleves he possessed. Besides,' he continued, ' she had a scar on her forehead which I remember perfectly —because it was a circumstance which struck me— having heard my mother describe how this scar had been produced by a heavy pair of tailor's shears which she had one day thrown at her sister's head.'

A short time afterwards the Elector received a letter written by one Fritz Dietrich from Leipzig, who informed him that he had learnt that a person, whose description he gave, was at Rossla, adding that he must be on his guard against her as she had already played tricks upon the Elector of Brandenburg and the Duke of Silesian-Leignitz. She had also been found out several times in acts of swindling.

The Elector does not appear to have taken the warning seriously, for shortly after he sent the ' Duchess Anne ' a ring and agreed to provide apartments for her, two women, a maid, and a lackey in the Palace of Grimmenstein at Gotha.

Anne acknowledged the Elector's kindness and sealed her letter with an impression of the arms of Juliers Cleves. This was followed by another document in which she secured all her jewels and treasures to the Elector and his brother and expressed her intention of making further large gifts to other members of the family.

In this way she continued to impose on the Elector, who seems to have been quite convinced that her stories were genuine and her statements true.

At length, however, clever and cunning though she undoubtedly was, she made a false step which led to her undoing. Among other treasures which she declared she possessed was a barrel of gold which she asserted she had deposited in the Town Hall at Nuremburg. On the instructions of the Elector a *jäger* was despatched to the city to get the barrel, but when he asked for it the young bailiff in charge failed to understand him. The Elector's agent at Nuremburg also wrote to him stating that the City Council had no knowledge of such a barrel of gold.

This appears to have at last aroused the Elector's

suspicions and he gave orders to the Commandant Mila not to allow Anne to leave the Castle of Grimmenstein. He was also instructed to demand repayment of the money that had been advanced to her. The climax came at the end of July, when an envoy arrived from the Duke of Juliers demanding the arrest of the ' Duchess Anne.'

She was brought before Dr. Stephen Clodius, the ducal councillor, by John Luther and the collector of taxes of the city of Gotha. On being questioned she first firmly adhered to all her stories, but after being removed to the Castle of Tenneberg for further interrogation she threw herself on her knees and begged for mercy. But although she retracted her previous statements she began to fabricate fresh ones.

The result of her examination was reported to Juliers, and her final story, that she was a natural daughter of Duke John of Cleves by Margaret von Schenk, a nun of the convent of Eisen, was proved to be entirely false.

The executioner of Jena was then dispatched to Tenneberg to be present at the next examination of the prisoner, who was threatened with torture if she did not speak the truth. This only brought forth a new story from Anne, who now declared that ' a demon was the cause of her fabrications and she had had many struggles with him.'

Tired of her procrastination, the court decided to hand her over to the executioner to be put on the rack. Before this was carried out one of the judges noticed that the prisoner's arms were covered with spots which Anne alleged had been caused by the ' demon who had terribly bruised them.' This, together with her claim that she was a daughter, though a natural one, of the house of Cleves, saved her from torture, and she was ordered to be taken back to Tenneberg.

With tears in her eyes she implored the Elector to pardon her. ' She asked for a priest to console her, a barber with ointment to dress her wounds, and begged she might be constantly watched in case the " demon " visited her again.'

She was again confined in the Castle of Tenneberg, and it is recorded that ' on Sundays she was allowed to have roast meat and wine.' Books were provided for her amusement and she was well cared for during her imprisonment.

This is the last heard of the mysterious impersonator who claimed to be Anne of Cleves. That she was a remarkably clever adventuress is shown from some of her letters, which are still kept in the library of Gotha. Besides the Elector, John Frederick, it is evident she had been in correspondence with the Elector Joachim of Brandenberg, Duke Frederick of Holstein, and the Duke of Silesian-Leignitz, all of whom addressed her as ' The High and Noble Lady Anne, born Duchess of Juliers and Cleves, crowned Queen of England, our very dear and greatly honoured cousin.'

The real identity of this woman has never been established. That she had an intimate knowledge of the noble families with which she claimed kinship is proved by her letters, and it has been suggested that she was probably one of the bedchamber women to Anne of Cleves who came to England with her and so was well acquainted with her ways.

ALTHOUGH she generally carried on her activities in the garb of her own sex, Mary Carleton was one of the most daring and cunning impersonators of her time. During her remarkable career she did not hesitate to commit the most barefaced frauds and robberies to gain her own ends, the chief object of which was to obtain possession of money.

She is said to have been born in Canterbury, where her father sang in the choir of the Cathedral. From girlhood she showed a volatile and lively disposition and delighted in reading stories of romance and adventure. Before she was twenty she married a journeyman shoemaker and had two children by him who died in infancy. She proved both reckless and extravagant, and as she found her husband was unable to give her sufficient money to spend on clothes and luxuries, she left him and set out to seek her fortune.

She had the advantage of good looks and a fine figure which, combined with a fascinating manner, enabled her to become friends with people above her station in life. She made her way from Canterbury to Dover where she established herself and formed an acquaintance with a surgeon practising in that town. He became an ardent admirer, and it was not long before he proposed to her and on her acceptance they were married. Her legal husband, on hearing this shortly afterwards, gave information and she was arrested and tried at Maidstone on a charge of committing bigamy. Owing to some technicality, she was acquitted and, having gathered sufficient money, she left this country for Holland and travelled from thence to Cologne. On her arrival in Germany, by selling what valuables she had been able to carry away, she amassed a considerable sum and, taking handsome lodgings, she cut a dashing figure in the city on the Rhine.

Tiring of Cologne she went on to Spa, where she soon made friends, among whom was a wealthy old man who had a large estate in the neighbourhood. He became infatuated with her and presented her with valuable jewellery and a gold medal and chain which had been given to him when serving under Count Tilly. At length he pressed her to marry him ; Mary coyly asked for time to consider his proposal, but later consented to ' make him happy in three days time.' The old man, who was transported with delight, meanwhile showered gifts upon her and liberally supplied her with money for the wedding.

Mary now made plans for a retreat and, with the assistance of her landlady, to whom she had made valuable presents from the jewellery she had received from the doting old man, she packed all her belongings and prepared to leave. She sent the landlady to engage a seat in a coach which took a different road from that to Cologne, and after she had left the house, broke open the box in which she kept her valuables, took the contents, and immediately set off in a hired carriage for Utrecht.

From thence she travelled to Amsterdam, where she sold her gold medal and chain together with some of the jewels, and made her way to Rotterdam, where she took a passage for England.

She landed in London at Billingsgate early one morning at the end of March in 1663 and, finding no other accommodation available, she took a room at the Exchange Tavern, where she gave herself out as ' a princess ' who had just arrived from Germany.

The presence of a handsome and fashionably

dressed woman in a tavern chiefly frequented by men naturally made a stir, and a number of them soon fell victims to her charms. She resolved to take advantage of their attentions and solicitude for her welfare, and one day, while surrounded by admirers in the general room, she burst into tears and told them a pathetic story of how she, a ' German princess,' had fallen into reduced circumstances. She informed them that her father was Lord Henry Vandwolway, a ' Prince of the Empire,' and she had been compelled to take refuge in England. The whole company was touched with compassion on hearing her story, which she related with such simplicity and pathos that they at once made a collection among themselves and gave her all the money they could muster, with a promise of more to follow. The ' German princess ' now became a centre of attraction and received many gifts from the frequenters of the tavern, including the landlord. He became so fully convinced of her rank and standing that he introduced her to his brother-in-law, one John Carleton, who soon began to pay his addresses to the stately and beautiful visitor.

At first the somewhat haughty princess appeared to resent his attentions, but later she began to receive him more graciously, and at length he came to believe himself the happiest of men. He made her an offer of marriage, which, after a little hesitation, in order to show the honour she was doing him, she accepted.

Shortly after the wedding had taken place Mr. King the landlord received a letter which stated that the woman who was residing at his house and who had recently been married to his brother-in-law was an impostor, and that she already had two husbands living and had made off from the last with all the money she could lay her hands on.

Mr. Carleton put the matter in the hands of the

authorities, who, after finding that the accusations were true, arrested the ' Princess ' and she was prosecuted and charged with bigamy, but, again owing to lack of evidence, she was acquitted.

Mary then resolved to try her fortune on the stage and succeeded in getting an engagement after telling stories of the great figure she had cut in Society abroad. She appeared in several plays with success, including one called the ' German Princess,' in which she played the principal part. Her handsome appearance, wit, and captivating manner brought her many admirers, among them two young men of wealth and fashion who were ready to lay their riches at her feet. She encouraged them for a time, but after getting three hundred pounds from each, she chided them with having the impudence to make love to a princess, and sent them about their business.

Her next victim was a wealthy old gentleman who, although he knew something of her chequered career, offered her a hundred a year if she would consent to be his mistress. After he had made her some generous gifts she accepted his proposal and took up her residence at his house. He loaded her up with costly presents, and all went well until one evening he was brought home quite intoxicated after taking too much wine. When she had seen him safely asleep Mary rifled his pockets and found a bill for a hundred pounds and some loose money. Taking these she discovered the key of his cash-box and emptied it, and, with the contents, together with a valuable gold watch, she left the house.

She then took lodgings, and when she presented the bill, as the acceptor knew her, she received the cash at once.

Settled in her new abode, she gave out that she was a lady who had just come into a thousand pounds, and whose father was able to give her twice that sum,

but she had left his house and did not want her
whereabouts discovered. The landlady of the house
believed her story and having a nephew whom she
thought might be a suitable partner for the wealthy
young lady, introduced him as a new boarder. She
made him known to Mary and he soon fell a victim to
her charms. He presented her with a gold watch
which she accepted after some show of reluctance,
and later he became her lover. One day when they
were together there was a knock at the door and a
porter handed in a letter. Mary tore it open and,
after glancing at the contents, cried out, ' I am
ruined ! I am ruined ! ' and then apparently swooned
away.

The young man sprang to her assistance, lifted her
up in his arms, and laid her on a couch. This soon
brought her round, and when she had composed
herself, she said, ' Since you are at last acquainted
with most of my concerns I shall not make a secret
of this. Read this letter for yourself and you will
know.'

The communication, which had been concocted by
Mary, who had arranged for its delivery by the porter,
was a long one and was signed, ' Your sincere friend.
S.E.' It stated that her brother had died and left her
all he had, besides which, with her father's estate of
two hundred a year, to which she was heir, she would
have a considerable income. Her father was preparing
to come to London to find her, and if she was not
ready to submit to his commands it would be advisable
for her to change her residence. The young man, after
reading this, at once agreed it would be best for her to
leave the lodgings, and he would hide her in the
apartments he had formerly occupied which he was
proud to place at her disposal. She accepted with
gratitude and, taking her maid with her, she drove
away to the address he gave her. She found the suite

of rooms beautifully furnished and very comfortable, but after exploring them and finding a desk which contained a bag with a hundred pounds in it, she decided to leave early in the morning. She found two suits of men's clothes. Mary dressed herself in one and the maid in the other, and after coiling their hair under suitable hats discovered in a cupboard, they sauntered forth and got safely away.

As soon as they were established in new lodgings over a mercer's shop in Cheapside, Mary called on a French weaver in Spitalfields and ordered goods to the value of forty pounds. As she had not the money with her to pay, the weaver went with her to her lodgings in a carriage to receive it. She asked him in and told him to sit down and make out his account, half of which was to be charged to a lady friend who was in another room. Then she left him, taking the silk with her to show the friend. After a while, the maid brought in a bottle of wine which she placed before the weaver and told him to help himself. Minutes went by and he still sat patiently waiting, but no one came for nearly an hour. At length, his patience having been exhausted, he called upon the landlady to know the reason. She informed him that the ' Princess ' had left as she had only taken the rooms temporarily.

Mary, meanwhile, had transferred herself to some lodgings in the house of a tailor whom she at once engaged to make up the silk she had stolen from the Spitalfields weaver. The tailor, convinced that he had got a rich lodger, soon made up all the material into the dresses she required.

One day she told him that she intended holding a grand party, and she gave his wife a pound to procure what was necessary for the guests, promising to pay the balance the next day.

On the night of the party a generous supply of

refreshments was provided with plenty of wine. The tailor and his wife did themselves so well that they had to retire to bed early. This was just what Mary wanted, for when the guests (who were all thieves) were departing, each was carrying a silver tankard, a bowl, or some other valuable article, and the maid had packed all the clothes she could find. The moment they got into the street, all the booty was put into a coach into which they got and were driven off to an unknown address.

During her impersonation of the ' German Princess,' Mary had acquired some very fine sables, and arrayed in them she next took rooms in Fuller's Rents, Holborn. Soon after she had established herself there she sent for a young lawyer in Gray's Inn to come and see her. She told him that owing to the recent death of her father she had inherited a large fortune, but she was married to an extravagant husband from whom she was separated. He had resolved to secure it for himself and had threatened to prosecute her. What should she do ?

While she was relating this story to the lawyer, a woman ran upstairs and dashing into the room cried : " Oh, Madame, we are undone ! My master is below asking for you and swears he will come up to your chamber."

" Oh, heavens ! " Mary exclaimed. " What shall I do ? "

" Why ? " asked the astonished lawyer.

" Why ? " she echoed. " I was thinking of you and what excuse I could make ! He is insanely jealous ! Step into this closet until I can send him away."

The surprised young man immediately got into the closet and Mary locked the door. He had no sooner got inside when he heard a man loudly demanding admission to the room. The moment he entered he heard him thunder : " Madame, I understand you have a man in your room. A pretty companion for an innocent woman. Where is the villain ? Let me see him or you will be the first victim."

He then made a dash at the closet door, burst it open, and there stood the mystified lawyer trembling in every limb. The husband drew his sword and the young man thought his last hour had come. But Mary intervened, and calling for help, a strange man came in and helped her to seize the irate husband and disarm him. Nothing but blood or an adequate sum of money, he declared, could wipe out his wife's disgrace. The lawyer protested and related the whole story of how he had been sent for by the lady. Then the kind stranger who had entered and helped to seize the enraged man proposed arbitration, and he thought the lawyer should pay the husband at least five hundred pounds. The lawyer refused, but after some discussion, thinking that the situation if it became known would be seriously detrimental to his professional standing, agreed to hand over one hundred pounds. He at once wrote a note to a friend in his office to send the money, and after it had arrived and he had paid it over he was allowed to depart.

Not long after this episode, Mary was arrested and charged with stealing ten silver tankards in Covent Garden from shops in Milford-lane and Lothbury. She was taken to Newgate, tried, convicted, and sentenced to transportation to Jamaica.

In two years' time she managed to escape and return to London. After obtaining some money from her friends she again established herself in fine apartments and assumed the character of a wealthy woman. She became acquainted with a rich apothecary who fell to her blandishments and speedily married her, but in a very short time she decamped, taking with her three hundred pounds of his money.

Her next move was to take rooms at the house of a watchmaker at Charing Cross. Having ingratiated herself with the landlord and his wife, she invited them one night to go and see a play at the Duke's Theatre and provided them with tickets. They went off delighted and in their absence she stripped the shop of watches and jewellery to the value of six hundred pounds and disappeared.

Retribution, however, came at last and put an end to her career of crime in a curious manner. A Mr. Freeman, a brewer, had been robbed of two hundred pounds, and suspicion fell on Mary. The police went to search her house one night and entered a bedroom where they found Mary in her nightgown. On the table they caught sight of two letters laying open and noticed they were signed 'Mary Carleton.' They recognized the name and took her off to Newgate on suspicion. When she was questioned and asked if she went by the name of Mary Carleton, she replied ' Yes.' On inquiries it was found she had escaped from custody in Jamaica and still had time to serve.

She was indicted and charged with stealing a piece of gold in Chancery Lane and was found guilty and sentenced to death. She pleaded that she was with child, but this was disproved by a jury of matrons who examined her. A date was fixed for her execution at Tyburn. Meanwhile she was visited in prison by many people who were anxious to see a woman, who, though only thirty-eight, had had such an extraordinary career and who in her frauds had shown remarkable cunning and ingenuity.

On the day she went to the gallows, she pinned a portrait of her husband (which husband is not recorded) on her sleeve and, escorted by a friend named Mr. Crouch, took her place in the cart. On the way through St. Giles they stopped at a tavern and Mary regaled herself with a pint of canary. After addressing the great crowd which had assembled, she was hanged on 22 January 1673. Next day her friends took her body in a coach and she was buried in St. Martin's Churchyard.

IMPOSTURE, with the object of obtaining titles, estates, and wealth, has raised disputes and trials from time to time throughout the centuries, and among the more notable cases of the kind was the claim made by a woman to the estates of the Earldom of Derwentwater in 1868.

This person based her claim on being a descendant of James Radcliffe, the third Earl of Derwentwater who was executed at Tower Hill after the rebellion. When he was twenty-three he married Anna Maria, a daughter of Sir John Webb of Carford, Dorset, and by her he had one son, John Radcliffe, and a daughter, who afterwards married the eighth Lord Petre.

Having embraced the Jacobite cause James was sent to the Tower and, in 1716, he was executed, and the whole of his large estates were confiscated and given absolutely by the Crown to Greenwich Hospital.

But, it was asserted by the Act of Attainder, that the property belonging to forfeited persons was vested in the Crown only and the Earl, having only a life interest in the estates, could forfeit no further interest. His only son, therefore, lost his title, but was admitted tenant entail of all the settled seats, and of these he was in possession for sixteen years. It was alleged that the reported death of John Radcliffe, the son of the last Earl, was a scheme on the part of his friend to protect him from his Hanoverian enemies. It was stated that he had died at the home of his grandfather, Sir John Webb, then living in Great Marlborough Street, London. Others said he was killed by a fall from his horse when in France and that his interment was a sham to facilitate his escape from France to Germany, where he was supposed to have married the Countess of Waldsteine-Wates and, bearing her name, to have died at the age of eighty-six.

By this reputed marriage he is said to have had a son called John James Anthony Radcliffe who married a descendant of John Sobieski of Poland. It was their daughter Amelia who laid claim to the Derwentwater estates in 1868.

In furtherance of her claim, which was not entertained, she determined to seize the family seat of Dilstone Castle, and the story of her attempt to occupy the ancient ruin is thus told.

One morning at the end of September 1868, much excitement was caused in the quiet village of Dilstone by the appearance at the gate of the old Castle of a person wearing an Austrian military uniform, armed with a sword and other equipment, and mounted on a pony.

The leader was accompanied by a number of retainers and a wagon stacked with furniture and other goods, which they at once began to unload and carry into the partly ruined building. Few of the rooms had ceilings, but tarpaulins were soon fixed up to serve as a protection from wind and rain. The uniformed leader gave out that she was Amelia, Countess of Derwentwater, who had come to take possession of the home of her ancestors.

The account of the occupation of the castle is given in various letters she wrote to her friends at the time, and published in her ' Diary,' the first of which is dated 29 September 1868.

' Here I am, my dear friend, at my own home, my roofless home, and my first scrawl from here is to the vicarage. You will be sorry to hear that the

Lords of Her Majesty's Council have defied all equitable terms in my eleven years suffering case.

' My counsel and myself have only received impertinent replies from under-officials. Had my Lords met my case like gentlemen and statesmen, I should not have been driven to the course I intend to pursue.

' I left the Terrace very early this morning, and at half-past seven I arrived at the carriage road of Dilstone Castle. Before me lay the ruins of my grandfather's baronial castle ; my heart beat more quickly as I approached. I am attended by two faithful retainers, Michael and Andrew. Mr. Samuel Aiston conveyed a few useful things ; the gentle and docile pony trotted on until I reached the level top of the carriage road and then we stopped. I dismounted and opened the gate and bade my squires to follow, and in the front of the old flag-tower I cut with a spade 30 square feet of green sod and Michael placed some of it in my hands. I then daringly climbed up the broken staircase and formed this green sod into a barrier for my feet in the once happy nursery, the mother's joyful upstairs parlour, the only room now standing, and quite roofless. I found no voice to cheer me, nothing but naked plasterless walls, a hearth with no frame of iron. The little chapel contains the sacred tombs of the dead and the dishonoured ashes of my grandsires.

' But here is the land, the house of my fathers which I have been robbed of ; this is a piece of the castle and the room in which they lived and talked and walked and smiled and were cradled and watched with tender affection.

' Radclyffe's flag is once more raised, and the portraits of my grandfather and great-grandfather with me here back again in Devilstone Castle (alias

Dilstone), and hang on each side of this roofless room where both their voices once sounded.

'Twelve o'clock of the same day. My tears of excitement have yielded to counter-excitement. I have just had an intrusive visitor who came to inquire if it was my intention to stay here.

'I replied in the affirmative, adding earnestly, "I have come to my roofless home," and asked "Who are you?"

'He answered, "I am Mr. Grey, the agent for Her Majesty, and I shall have to communicate your intention."

'I answered, "Quite right, Mr. Grey. Then what title have you to show that Her Majesty has a right here to my freehold estates?"

'He replied, "I have no title."

'I then took out a parchment with the titles and the barony and manors and the names of my forty-two rich estates and held it before him and said, "I am the Countess of Derwentwater and my title and claim are acknowledged and substantiated by the Crown of England morally, legally, and officially and therefore my title is the title to these forty-two estates."

'He has absented himself quietly.'

On 30 September she again wrote :

'Since yesterday a star has darkened in my earthly horizon. You will scarcely believe your ears, but indeed it is true. I myself and both my men are made prisoners on my own ground. Mr. Grey, the agent, has shut all the gates of the castle, and they are to be locked. I have to open for myself. I am anxious about my men, but they smile at Mr. Grey's folly and usurped authority.

'Some kind friends came this morning with

stores and provisions, but they were not allowed to enter. The man Glover, a little sub-agent paid out of my estate, acts as gaoler and keeper of our prison and I hear Mr. Grey has placed the wood-man and other sublime monsters at the entrance of all the gates.

' Our lands were not confiscated, but they were unlawfully seized because the male heirs of the cruelly decapitated James, third Earl of Derwent-water, would not sign the oath of Abjuration.

' I feel weak and ill this morning. I am cold and do not dare to sleep. I have no maid with me. I could not ask the meanest peasant girl to share with me the discomfort of this roofless home.'

On 1 October she wrote :

' My men say, the agent Grey has sent over some breakfast on this third day, but I can neither give nor take quarter from Her Majesty's agents of my estates. I have had no warm food and the water from the river does not taste good. Rest quite happy, though I am very ill with cold.'

On the same day she again wrote :

' All my friends have been turned back and I am told no letters are to be sent.'

2 October :

' I have been told I am a trespasser, but have committed no crime against my title. Nevertheless, I have been dragged out of my grandfather's castle by brute force and placed on this road, a spectacle of barbarity. If you could have been a witness of these pitiful cowards attacking a defenceless lady, and the dingy Grey man directing these savages !

O would that my noble brother had been living !
He would have drawn his sword upon each lawless
coward in this horrible scene.'

Amelia, when expelled from the castle, encamped
on the road outside while a tent was rigged up to
shelter her, and her next letter is dated from ' Dilstone
carriage road,' in October 1868. In this she tells her
friend she had received at daybreak a wooden pavilion,
4 ft. 8 in. broad and 17 ft. long, with a good window
and a nice room for servants.

' This,' she writes, ' is a real act of Christian
humanity and comes from a chosen few of the
Rev. John Wesley's disciples to whom I am a
perfect stranger. I never did anything for the
Wesleyans, but this act of humanity does all credit
to the great Wesley's teaching of the Bible.

' It is very remarkable that it is on the old deer
park where this little camp stands and the ground
where the Reverend Wesley held his great camp
meeting with the thousands of people he gathered
out of the lanes and streets in Hexhamshire when
he went down to form circuits for travelling
preachers in the county of Northumberland.'

After being left unmolested for about three weeks
in her wooden hut by the roadside, action was taken
against Amelia by Grey, the agent, at the Quarter
Sessions for the county of Northumberland.

On 21 October, the chief constable was questioned
about the strange state of affairs in the district, and
he reported that as the encampment was a little way
from the highway, the lady could not be apprehended
under the Vagrant Act. A summons was, however,
taken out by the local surveyor, and when the case
was heard Amelia was convicted, but she appealed
to the Court of Queen's Bench. The appeal went

against her, but meanwhile the cold weather set in and drove the lady from her temporary abode. In the spring she again appeared to resume her fight, and this time took possession of a cottage at Dilstone. On 17 November 1869, while Mr Grey, the agent, was collecting the Derwentwater rents, Amelia marched into his office accompanied by her retainers and forbade the proceedings. She was again dressed in her military uniform richly decorated with gold braid, which caused a crowd to gather outside and they cheered her loudly when she left.

About this time she published a book which was entitled, *Jottings from my diary and the journal of my grandfather John, fourth Earl of Derwentwater.* In it she drew attention to her claim and the reasons for supporting it.

A sympathizer commenting on it says : ' The Countess in her person expresses all that is dignified, and she excels in the variety of attitude and the expression of sentiment. She is a clever artist and knows how to blend dignity and sweet serenity. It is much to be regretted that the heiress of Derwentwater, a lady of birth, talent, and education and descended from one of the oldest, richest, and noblest patriots on English records, should have met with such barbarous treatment from the rulers of her country in the reign of the gentle Queen Victoria in 1868.

' It is appalling to see a defenceless lady struggling for her father's home with lawless tyrants in the year 1868, and martyred simply for asking for her lawful rights. It would be impossible for us to convey the least idea of the bitter suffering and torture which has been extracted by Government on the much-wronged heiress of Derwentwater.

' We blush to hear ourselves justly upbraided by foreigners who came far and wide to Dilstone Castle in October 1868, to be eyewitnesses of England's barbarities to a Radclyffe, the lonely heiress of Derwentwater.'

In her book Amelia prints the letters written from the Tower of London in February 1716 by James, the third Earl of Derwentwater, to his wife, Anna.

On 5 January 1870 Amelia again returned to the charge, and a great demonstration was organized on her farm at Consett, Co. Durham. A few days previously she had seized a quantity of live-stock on another farm for rent she alleged to be due to her, but an injunction was obtained to prevent her selling it. However, she defied the law, and in the midst of a great uproar the cattle was sold, flags were waved, and speeches made by the claimant's supporters.

This roused the Lords of the Admiralty and they took action and formally announced that the claims of the pseudo-Countess were frivolous. They warned tenants on the estate against paying any rents to her and summoned those who had assisted at the sale. But in spite of all this opposition Amelia remained undaunted, and in the following February made another attempt to collect the rents of the forty-two farms on the estates which, she persisted in declaring, belonged to her. Bailiffs were called in to resist her efforts to levy on property, and succeeded in preventing them.

On 11 February 1870 the Lords of the Admiralty applied for an injunction to prevent Amelia from entering the Greenwich estates. Their application was granted and some of her supporters were summoned and sentenced to short terms of imprisonment.

Amelia Radclyffe was not without friends and had a staunch supporter in Countess Marie Mouravieff. When she became short of money she declared she had jewels, pictures, and documents stored in Germany, but was penniless and unable to go and fetch them. A sympathizer then came forward and advanced her £2000 on loan in order to go to Germany and bring them to this country. Amelia went and brought them, but they proved to be of little value and insufficient to satisfy her creditors.

In the end, in order to meet their immediate demands, the jewels and pictures were brought to the hammer in an auction-room at Hexham, and afterwards Amelia Radcliffe, who claimed to be Countess of Derwentwater, disappeared from the public eye and abandoned her long fight to recover the estates.

WILLIAM, fourth Earl of Wicklow, died without male issue ; his next brother, the Reverend Francis Howard, had died during the Earl's lifetime after being married twice. By his first marriage he had three sons, all of whom died, but he had another son by his second wife who claimed the peerage on his uncle's death. A rival to the estates however appeared in the person of William George Howard, an infant, who was stated to be the son of William George Howard, the eldest son of the Reverend Francis Howard, by his first marriage to a Miss Ellen Richardson.

The birth of this child was disputed by the original claimant and the question was referred to the House of Lords. On investigation it transpired that William George, the reputed father of the child, was married to a Miss Richardson in February 1863, and four months after the marriage went to lodge with a Mrs. Bloor at 27 Burton Street, Eaton Square. They went away after three weeks and on returning to London at the end of the year, tried to procure their old apartments in Burton Street.

The house was however full, but rooms were obtained for Mrs. Howard at No. 32 in the same street. Mr. Howard did not reside there himself, but used to meet his wife occasionally in a room at No. 27. A little later, Mrs. Howard was able to return to No. 27 and again lodged at the Bloors', occupying the entire upper portion of the house, the lower part being rented by one of her friends named Baudenave.

Meanwhile, Mr. Howard was in Ireland. Mr. Bloor went to see him in May 1864 and told him that Mrs. Howard was expecting a child, and it was agreed that she should remain on in Burton Street until her confinement was over.

On 16 May, Mrs. Howard informed the Bloors that she intended to go away, and leaving the house she took a cab to the station. She returned, however, in a short time, declaring that she felt ill, and was at once put to bed.

When Mr. Bloor returned from his work he decided to call in a Dr. Wilkins by Mrs. Howard's special request. The doctor lived some distance away and Mr. Bloor went for him, but at 9.30 p.m. when he returned without him, he was told by his wife that Mrs. Howard had been safely delivered of a son. Glad to be spared another long journey Mr. Bloor did not go out again and Dr. Wilkins was not summoned until several weeks had passed, when he called and saw Mrs. Howard and prescribed for the baby for some slight ailment.

Mrs. Bloor (who had attended Mrs. Howard), Miss Rose Day (her sister), Miss Jane Richardson (sister of Mrs. Howard), and Mr. Baudenave (who lodged in the other part of the house), all said they repeatedly saw the child during the following three months, although its existence appears to have been kept a secret from everyone else.

At the inquiry, it was contended for the original claimant that the story told concerning the baby was so shrouded in mystery as to be absolutely incredible.

The evidence of Dr. Wilkins could not be obtained as he had died in the meantime and it was asserted that the whole story of the birth of the child had been concocted by Baudenave, who had been lodging in the house. He had now disappeared and could not be found. He was stated to have been living on terms of suspicious intimacy with Mrs. Howard.

In the evidence called to show the birth had not taken place, two doctors declared they had attended a lady who they swore was Mrs. Howard, and there was nothing to prove she had ever had a child.

When the case was resumed on 1 March 1870, Sir Roundell Palmer (Lord Selborne), who represented Charles Francis Howard, the original claimant, made a most extraordinary statement which gave a new complexion to the romantic story. He told the court that he was in a position to prove that in August 1864 Mrs. Howard and another lady visited a workhouse in Liverpool and procured a newly born child from its mother, who was called Mary Best. Three nurses were called to prove this assertion, two of whom swore to Mrs. Howard's identity and that she had taken the baby away with her.

At the next sitting a week later Mrs. Howard appeared, but refused to be sworn until the witnesses who were to be brought against her had been first examined. As she persisted in her refusal, after being warned, she was committed for contempt of court. Towards the close of the sitting a dramatic turn was given to the proceedings by the receipt of a telegram from Boulogne stating that the real person who had bought and taken possession of Mary Best's baby had been found and was ready to come foward at the next hearing.

Great interest was excited the day the case was resumed and all awaited the arrival of the important witnesses from Boulogne, but none put in an appearance.

Mary Best was however there to give evidence and admitted she had left the workhouse with a baby which she had passed off as her own. She declared that this child was given to her while she was in the workhouse ward, but she did not know the name of the mother or the person who gave it to her. This child had since died and her relatives could prove it.

On 31 March 1870, the court delivered its judgment and the Lord Chancellor announced that their Lordships had come to the conclusion that Charles Francis Howard had made out his claim to the Earldom of Wicklow and that the infant claimant, said to be the son of Mrs. Howard, had failed in establishing a claim. Although two witnesses had stated they were present when the alleged birth took place, he could give no credence to the story. It was inconsistent with all the admitted facts, and he had arrived at the conclusion it was a mere fabrication.

The evidence of Dr. Baker Brown, who had identified Mrs. Howard as the person he had examined on 8 July 1864 and who stated she had never had a child, was very emphatic. The Liverpool story was certainly very extraordinary, in view of the fact that Mary Best was delivered of a *fair* child and the baby she took with her when she left the workhouse was *dark*. Strange though it was, this fact had no bearing on the case.

Lord Chelmsford, in agreeing with the Lord Chancellor, remarked it was impossible to disbelieve the story of the alleged birth without coming to the conclusion that certain of the witnesses had been guilty of conspiracy and perjury.

The Earl of Winchelsea gave his opinion that the story of Mrs. Howard was utterly incredible and worthy to form the plot of a sensational novel. He regretted that Mr. Baudenave, the principal mover in the conspiracy, had escaped unscathed. Their Lordships resolved that Mrs. Howard's child had no claim to the Earldom.

Thus ended this strange and romantic case which in some respects was said to be without precedent in legal history.

XXXIII

IN 1866 the strange case of Mrs. Ryves, daughter of a lady who assumed the title of Olive, Princess of Cumberland, excited great interest throughout the country. Together with her son William Henry Ryves, she claimed to be the legitimate daughter of John Thomas Serres and Olive his wife, and that the mother of Mrs. Ryves was the legitimate daughter of Henry Frederick, Duke of Cumberland, and Olive Wilmot his wife, who were married by Dr. Wilmot in Grosvenor Square, London, at the house of Lord Archer, on 4 March 1767.

According to the story revealed at the trial, Olive Wilmot was the daughter of a Dr. James Wilmot, a country clergyman and fellow of an Oxford college. During his time at the University, Wilmot had made the acquaintance of Count Poniatowski, who eventually became King of Poland, and through him had been introduced to his sister, a girl of great beauty. She fell in love with young Wilmot and married him and later a baby was born who, as she grew up, inherited her mother's good looks and developed into a lovely girl. Wilmot had to keep his marriage secret, especially in Oxford, as he did not wish to lose his fellowship. His daughter was called Olive and in 1767, when she was seventeen and was staying with Lord Archer in Grosvenor Square, she was introduced to the Duke of Cumberland, the younger brother of King George III. He fell in love with her and very shortly afterwards they were married, on 4 March 1767, the ceremony being performed by Dr. James Wilmot, the girl's father.

251

The marriage took place at nine o'clock in the evening, and the only persons present were Lord Brooke (afterwards Lord Warwick) and Mr. J. Addey. Two formal certificates were drawn up and signed by Dr. Wilmot, Lord Brooke and Mr. Addey. These certificates were verified by those of Lord Chatham and Mr. Dunning (who afterwards became Lord Ashburton).

The Duke of Cumberland and his wife lived together for four years, but in October 1771, when she was expecting a child, the Duke left her and is said to have then contracted a bigamous marriage with Lady Anne Luttrel.

The King, George III, when told of the marriage of his brother to Olive Wilmot, was so incensed that he refused to allow the Duke to come to Court.

After her desertion, Olive gave birth to a child who was also called Olive and should have borne the title of Princess of Cumberland. The baby was baptized by Dr. Wilmot, her grandfather.

Although George III was irritated by the conduct of his brother, he was anxious to shield the Duke from the consequences of a bigamous marriage, and for that purpose directed Lord Chatham, Lord Warwick, and Dr. Wilmot to conceal the real parentage of the child, and instructed that she should be re-baptized as the daughter of her uncle, Robert Wilmot, whose wife had been delivered of a baby about the same time.

Dr. Wilmot consented on consideration that the King and other persons should be certified as witnesses, in order that at some future time she should be able to claim her proper position. Now, Dr. Wilmot is said to have been in possession of a secret which gave him a hold over the King, for in 1759 he had secretly married him to Hannah Lightfoot, while in 1762 he was publicly married to Princess Charlotte and thus, like the Duke of Cumberland, he had committed bigamy.

Meanwhile, the child Olive Wilmot was brought up in the family of her uncle, Robert Wilmot, who is said to have received an allowance of five hundred a year for her support from Lord Chatham. On 17 May 1773, the King made Olive, Duchess of Lancaster, as stated in the following pronouncement :

' GEORGE R.,

' We are hereby pleased to create Olive of Cumberland, Duchess of Lancaster and to grant our Royal authority for Olive our said niece to bear and use the title and arms of Lancaster should she be in existence at the period of our Royal demise.

' Given at our Palace of St. James, May 17 1773.

' CHATHAM,

' J. DUNNING.'

In 1772, the year before, Dr. Wilmot was appointed to the living of Barton-on-the-Heath, in Warwickshire, and his granddaughter Olive went to live with him and passed as his niece.

When she was about eighteen she became acquainted with an artist named Serres, who was a well-known painter and a member of the Royal Academy. They were married in 1791, but the union was not a happy one and before long a separation took place.

A daughter was born to Mrs. Serres in Liverpool where she went to live in 1797, and she eventually married and became Mrs. Ryves. Mrs. Serres was also a clever painter and was the author of several books.

In 1805, the mother and daughter, who were living together, were taken to Brighton by some influential friends, and while there obtained an introduction to the Prince of Wales, who afterwards became George IV.

In 1807 Dr. Wilmot died, and his papers, together

with all the documents relating to the secret marriages, passed into the hands of Lord Warwick.

Mrs. Serres during all this time is said to have been in complete ignorance of the secret of her birth and it was not until 1815, when Lord Warwick was taken seriously ill, that it was thought proper to communicate the facts to her. The documents and papers were placed in her hands and the Duke of Kent was also informed.

The documents and papers were numerous and contained 43 signatures of Dr. Wilmot, 16 of Lord Chatham, 32 of Lord Warwick, 12 of Mr. Dunning, 18 of the Duke of Kent, and 12 of King George III.

According to Mrs. Serres, they had been pronounced by an expert as genuine, and it was on their authenticity that Mrs. Ryves and her daughter based their claim in the High Court of Justice in 1866.

The case was heard before Lord Chief Justice Cockburn, Lord Chief Baron Pollok, Sir James Wilde, and a special jury.

The whole romantic story of the birth and life of the original Olive Wilmot and the subsequent events in her career were related by the counsel for Mrs. Ryves, the claimant, and she was called to give evidence.

Speaking of certain of the documents bearing the signatures of Lord Warwick and the Duke of Kent, she swore that after the death of the Duke of Kent and his father, the Duke of Sussex paid a visit to her mother and herself in order to examine the documents and was satisfied they were genuine.

In one of the letters produced in court, said to have been written by the Duke of Kent, there was an acknowledgment of the marriage of his father with Hannah Lightfoot and the legitimacy of the second Olive Wilmot, and a plea that the latter should maintain secrecy during the life of the King.

The Attorney-General on behalf of the Crown pronounced the story of the claimant as absurd and audacious. The Polish princess and her charming daughter were pure myths, as also the pretended marriage of King George III to Hannah Lightfoot.

He contended that Mrs. Serres, the mother of Mrs. Ryves, the claimant, was not altogether responsible for her actions. She had become known to some members of the Royal family and began by writing eccentric letters to the Prince of Wales in 1809. Her correspondence showed evidence of delusions and in one letter she imagined herself to have been seriously injured by the Duke of York, while in another she fancied someone was trying to poison her. Her letters were full of references to astrology, the result of her studies in the occult, and her belief in ghosts.

At first she had stated she was the daughter of the Duke of Cumberland and Mrs. Payne, a sister of Dr. Wilmot's. The claim of legitimate Royal birth had first been mentioned at a time of great excitement when the case of Queen Caroline was brought before the public. The internal evidence of the papers themselves proved that they were preposterous forgeries.

The Lord Chief Justice, in summing-up the facts of the case, said some of the documents bore the strongest internal evidence of their falsity. The first claim put forward by Mrs. Serres was that she was the illegitimate daughter of the Duke of Cumberland by Mrs. Payne, and the next that she was the daughter by an unmarried sister of Dr. Wilmot. She put forward her present claim declaring she was the offspring of a lawful marriage between the Duke and Olive, the daughter of Dr. Wilmot.

The jury in arriving at a verdict declared that they were not satisfied that Olive Serres, the mother of Mrs. Ryves, was the legitimate daughter of Henry Frederick,

Duke of Cumberland, and Olive his wife, and further, they were not satisfied that Henry Frederick, Duke of Cumberland, was lawfully married to Olive Wilmot on 4 March 1767.

Mrs. Ryves was non-suited and so this long and complicated case, which caused a great sensation at the time, came to an end, and the judges ordered the documents to be impounded.